With creativity and l
premier postmodern
ship and contempora
unchurched commur
istry of this gifted preacher, committed husband, and loving father.
—Rev. Dr. Otis Moss, III
Senior Pastor, Trinity United Church of Christ, Chicago, IL

Courage under Fire offers both the spiritual and theological tools
that are needed to survive in a fractured world filled with broken
relationships. Gibson's unique and courageous degree of trans-
parency surrounding his own marriage is enough to make anyone
pick up this book.
—Kimberly P. Johnson, Ph.D.
Assistant Professor of Communication, Tennessee State University

Eugene Gibson is determined to honor God in every area of his life
and ministry. He has discerned that great preaching is autobio-
graphical and that its passion is strengthened by skilled transparen-
cy. This book will liberate you to trust that the journey of faith
involves failing upward and that God extends grace and power to
our attempts to honor him in every area of OUR lives.
—Dr. William H. Curtis
Senior Pastor, Mt. Ararat Baptist Church, Pittsburgh, PA

Eugene Gibson's gift of homiletical craftsmanship comes through
in this volume of sermons. His experience of relationships both
personal and pastoral can be seen through the lens of his unique
sermonic style. What you will experience is Dr. Gibson's uncanny
ability to not only inspire us, but also empower us to change. This
book will be a blessing to its readers.
—Rev. Dr. Wm. Marcus Small
Senior Pastor, New Calvary Baptist Church, Norfolk, VA

It takes a bold and courageous voice to address real issues facing
today's relationships. In this series of sermons, Dr. Eugene Gibson,
Jr. offers a profoundly unique, practical, and powerfully transpar-
ent perspective on guarding the relationship flame. Couples that

read *Courage under Fire* should benefit from its content. I am pleased to recommend this invaluable resource.

—Dr. Gina M. Stewart
Senior Pastor, Christ Missionary Baptist Church, Memphis, TN

Some books are must-reads and THIS IS ONE! Dr. Gibson has done an amazing job of sensing the pulse of marriage and challenging us all to fight through the difficulties that come with simply living. Thank you, Dr. Gibson, for your *Courage under Fire*.

—Rev. Dr. John Eric Guns
Senior Pastor, St. Paul Baptist Church, Jacksonville, FL

With his eloquent verbal precision and his self-evident love for preaching that percolates the mind, body, and soul, Dr. Eugene Gibson gives inspiring messages to aspiring couples who want to build relationships that can withstand the heat of life's tests.

—Rev. Reggie Bell, Jr.
Pastor, Fresh Start Church, Charlotte, NC

Relationships are hard work. Harder still is the intentional reflection necessary to go inward in order to make the outward better! In *Courage under Fire*, Dr. Eugene Gibson intentionally acknowledges and addresses the underlying issues of the labors of love. This series of sermons should be used by the open and honest as a mirror and source of reflection in serious relationships!

—Rev. Reginald Williams, Jr.
Senior Pastor, First Baptist Church, University Park, IL

Good sermons are like good poems; when well-thought-out and well-crafted, they invite you back to them again and again. Dr. Geno Gibson knows the turn of a phrase can capture the heart of a matter. Geno is unsparing in his uncovering of the problems that plague relationships of all kind and is also generous in his Divine imaginative solutions. What a gift this book is, as is the man who offers it.

—Dr. Valerie Bridgeman
Hebrew Bible & Homiletics Scholar
Founding President & CEO of WomanPreach! Inc.

COURAGE
under FIRE

**Guarding the
Romantic Flame
from Life's
Fiery Issues**

EUGENE L. GIBSON, JR.
Foreword by Frank A. Thomas

MMGI
BOOKS

To my girlfriend, wife,
and soul mate of 22 years, Nicole,
and the beautiful daughters you blessed me with,
Trinity Essence and Taylor Emani.
With all I am and ever hope to be,
this is for you.
You are the air I breathe.

Published by MMGI Books, Chicago, IL 60636
www.mmgibooks.com

Courage under Fire: Guarding the Romantic Flame from Life's Fiery Issues
Copyright © 2013 by Eugene L. Gibson, Jr.

Bible quotations in this volume are from The Holy Bible, King James Version (KJV). Used by permission. All rights reserved. New International Version 1984 Holy Bible, New International Version®, NIV® Copyright © 1973, 1978, 1984 by Biblica, Inc.® Used by permission. All rights reserved worldwide.

Interior design by Wendy Ronga / Hampton Design Group

ISBN 978-1-939774-11-8
Printed in the U.S.A.

Foreword by Frank A. Thomas vi

Acknowledgments vii

Introduction xi

1. Unsung: The Story of Jacob 1

2. The Re-Education of Plastic Barbie 10

3. Menace to Society 20

4. Just a Lil Bit 28

5. It's Always Business; It's Never Personal 36

6. Desperate Housewives, and the Men Who
Make Them Desperate 44

7. Baby Mama Drama 52

8. Sleeping with the Enemy 59

9. Living Beyond My Violation
by Dr. Rosalyn Nichols 67

10. Waiting to Exhale: Savannah and
the Curse of Eve 76

11. Waiting to Exhale: Robin and the Painful Past
by Zedric K. Clayton, II 86

12. Waiting to Exhale: Bernadine and
the Love Hangover 96

13. Waiting to Exhale: Gloria and the Crisis
of Co-dependency 107

14. Love the Hurt Away 115

15. Courage under Fire 121

Foreword

Several weeks ago, I was asked by a very prominent preacher who were the new and upcoming voices in the country that needed to be heard. Immediately and without hesitation I replied, "Eugene L. Gibson, Jr. of Memphis, Tennessee."

I have known the Rev. Doctor Eugene L. Gibson, Jr. since he was in high school. His father, the Rev. Eugene Gibson Sr., mentored me and introduced me to his gifted son. From that time until now, we have built a deep and lasting relationship. He sought my counsel about the faint stirring of a preaching call in his life. We prayed together around his leaving the position of minister of music, attending seminary, and exploring pastoral ministry. I hired him for his first ministerial full-time clergy position. He grew rapidly in that position and quickly became the pastor of Olivet Fellowship Baptist Church, The Place of the Outpouring, of Memphis, Tennessee. I preached the installation service and, as we mentors like to say, "Installed him in the church." I needed assistance in the teaching of my preaching classes and, for ten years now, we have labored together in assisting preachers to improve their preaching craft, much to the point that he knows my material better than I do. An astute son is one who studies his father such that he knows what the father is doing and can explain it to the father to help the father understand what he is doing. Many of the sermons that you read in this book are steeped in the 21st-century version of the celebrative preaching model. I am proud to say that Gibson has mastered the model and taken it to the next level beyond that of Henry H. Mitchell and myself.

It is not only the mastering of the celebrative model that makes *Courage under Fire: Guarding the Romantic Flame from Life's Fiery Issues* so moving and profound; it is also the rich insights and stirring content. The sermons themselves cover a wide range of subjects, but the common thread is being able to persevere through tough days and occurrences (fiery issues) in life and in relationships. Very rarely do we honestly and forthrightly in the pulpit discuss the fires of life. Much of it gets smoothed over by talk of breakthrough, miracle, favor of the Lord, too blessed to be stressed, etc. Gibson charts new territory by allowing God to address the down-to-earth hurts and pains of people.

For example, my favorite sermon is "Unsung: The Story of Jacob." Aside from the absolutely much-needed critique of reality television, through the story of Jacob, Gibson shows all our addictions: that is, in his words, the excessive, repetitive use of pleasurable activities to cope with unmanageable internal conflict, pressure, and stress. He convinces us all that we are guilty of some kind of addictive behavior and stand in need of God's grace. Jacob wrestles with his addictions until God gives him a new name. And even though Jacob leaves the struggle with a limp, he blesses the place and calls it Peniel, "God's face." We can wrestle with our addictions and God will give us a new name, and even in our limping we can call the place "God's face."

I offer congratulations to my son, the Reverend Doctor Eugene L. Gibson, Jr., for this collection. Enjoy and be blessed by every sermon. Discover insights from the word of God that will change your life. I introduce to you Eugene L. Gibson, Jr. whom I am proud to call my son in the ministry.

—Frank A. Thomas

Acknowledgments

It has been said that if you have the ability to see farther and your view is clearer then most likely it is because you are standing on the shoulders of those who have gone before you. For me, this statement resonates with the purest of truth. If it had not been for the Lord's grace and mercy and God's use of human faculty I would not be here today. Countless people have sacrificed, given words of encouragement, given finances, and given opportunities to birth this book; to all of you I say with the deepest humility, Thank You.

To my late father, the Rev. Eugene L. Gibson, Sr., and my mother, Mildred L. Gibson, words are inadequate to say enough thanks. For the foundation of love, unending support, and unwavering faith—most of all for your introduction of me to Jesus Christ— the One Who makes all that we do possible, I say much obliged. I pray I make you proud.

To my siblings, William Darryl, the late Everett James, and Eugenia Lynelle, thanks so much for your love and for making life so real. I love you guys. Miss you, Bucky!

To my in-laws who have become my family, Mr. and Mrs. Arthur and Marilyn Bolton and Mr. Daryl and Rev. Michelle Robinson; thank you so much for bringing such a beautiful jewel into the world and for allowing her to be in my world. Thank you for loving our children like you do.

To Dr. Stirling Culp, my mentor in music and life since I was in seventh grade, the standard of excellence that you set in ministry and in life is one that I now carry as a badge of honor. The Kingdom Quality level of ministry and service that I try to give and train others to is a direct reflection of your impact on my life. I bless God for you.

To my Pastor, the Rev. Dr. Frank Anthony Thomas, and his family; I want to thank you for taking up the time to nurture a young, gifted, but wounded preacher and showing the compassion of our God to one who needed it so. When I asked you to mentor me after Dad's death I had no idea that God would facilitate such an unbelievable relationship. Thanks!

To the congregations of Mission of Faith Baptist Church, New Faith Baptist Church, and Mississippi Boulevard Christian Church; thanks for allowing me to practice ministry on you. You put up with the earliest and most fragmented of sermonic thoughts and loved me in spite of them. Thank you for enduring my sophomoric mistakes as I was learning ministry. Thanks to Pastor Agnes Denise Bell for your loving but stern leadership as it pertains to pastoral ministry. Your impact and influence on me is immeasurable. I would like to give a special thanks to Pastor Tyrone Crider, Mr. and Mrs. Precious and Phyllis Luster, and Mr. and Mrs. Glen and Linda Sessoms for the contributions that allowed me to stay in seminary. I only pray that you see the dividends of your investment.

To the members of one of God's favorite Places, The Place of the Outpouring, Olivet Fellowship Baptist Church, words cannot express how much I love you. You took a chance on an unproven young pastor and have whooped me, loved me, stretched me, prayed for me, covered me, and honored both my family and me. You have, over time, gone from rejection to rejoicing over the preaching gift that God has given me; you are even now responsive and running after the vision God has assigned us. Thanks for allowing me to be your Pastor and, more than that, allowing me to be me. I love you and there is absolutely nothing you can do about it. And, of course, I Speak Life to You!

Thanks to my closest friends in ministry whose encouragement, camaraderie, and challenges—in preaching through the years and even now—have made this book possible: Pastor Reginald Bell, Jr.; Pastor Walter Carter, III; Dr. Marcus Cosby; Dr. William Curtis; Pastor Martin Espinosa; Dr. John Guns; Dr. Freddie Haynes; Dr. Derrick Hughes; Dr. Otis Moss, III; Dr. Jasmine Sculark; Dr. Martha Simmons; Dr. Gina Marcia Stewart; Dr. F. Bruce Williams; Pastor Romell Williams, Jr.; and of course the Wolf Pack, Dr. William Marcus Small and Pastor Reginald Williams, Jr.

Last but not least, I want to thank Dr. Rosalyn Nichols and Pastor Zedric Clayton for being a part of this book. The sermons that you wrote fit perfectly into the jigsaw puzzle of this endeavor. I pray that, through this, God will give you opportunity and success at every place where your foot shall set.

Finally, to the God of all Glory and of Grace, without Whom there would be nothing written, said, sung, or preached by someone like me that would be worth anything. How I can I say thanks for the thing you have done for me . . . ? I simply say, To God Be the Glory for the things He has done!

Now, please enjoy *Courage under Fire*. . . .

Introduction

I knew the moment I saw her that she was to be my wife. As she and her best friend walked into the choir rehearsal of my father's South Side Chicago church, I knew she was the future Mrs. Gibson. In fact, upon seeing her I spoke to the young man sitting next to me of my vision and told him she was to be my wife. However, what I could not have known is that he was the reason for her appearance; she was there to meet him.

Needless to say that, though there has been a mixture of both fortunate and unfortunate events, with our 18th wedding anniversary quickly approaching, things worked out better for me than they did for him. However, it must be stated that in spite of the fact that when I first saw Nicole it felt like I had known her all of my life, in spite of the fact that after being her boyfriend now for 22 years I would still choose her again, and in spite of the fact that after the birth of two daughters and the losing of a third child she still looks amazing; protecting and preserving our marriage has been hard work. Unfortunately no one told us.

Think about it. When people think about meeting and beginning a relationship with their significant other, celebration and spring is in the air. Whether single or married, the newness of relationship is almost unmatched in its excitement. The reason for this excitement is that the couple, whether they are aware or not, has been set ablaze by love and they and others around them are enamored by the warmth and glow of the flame. They complete each other's sentences, every joke is funny, and they agree on what to get for take-out. They love to be with each other because care, compassion, and concern are the order of each day and there is no way that the freshness could ever stale or sour. In fact, others look up to this couple and brag about this couple, and their flame even becomes a model of the maintenance of the relationship flame.

The problem is that when people speak about keeping the flame of a couple's relationship lit, hardly ever do they discuss the fires of life. No one mentions the fact that the flames of hurt, pain, heartbreak, addiction, pornography, infidelity, baby mama drama, illness, and the like are smoldering close by. Not many are courageous enough to speak truthfully about how much work it takes to keep the flame lit. That is what this book is about.

Courage under Fire: Guarding the Romantic Flame from Life's Fiery Issues is a collection of inspiring messages that will help those in married and single relationships guard the romantic flame against the fiery issues of life. Focusing on God's power of love and healing, this collection of sermons will help people endure and overcome life's toughest challenges. I call it a collection because, though most of the sermons were written and preached by me, I have the distinct pleasure to introduce two voices, the Rev. Dr. Rosalyn Nichols and Pastor Zedric Clayton, who masterfully and uniquely weigh in on this subject.

The Rev. Dr. Rosalyn R. Nichols is the Senior Pastor of the Freedom's Chapel Christian Church in Memphis, Tennessee, and the founder of A More Excellent Way, which is a non-profit organization that brings awareness and advocacy for victims of domestic violence. She preached the sermon "Living Beyond My Violation" at a City Wide Women's Only Worship service at Olivet Fellowship/The Place of the Outpouring. Her voice represents our single sisters. Pastor Zedric K. Clayton, II, Senior Pastor of The City of Truth, Clarksdale, Mississippi, is a son of my ministry and served as volunteer, Associate Minister, and finally as the Youth Pastor of Olivet Fellowship/The Place of the Outpouring for over eight years. We used his voice to represent youth and young adults.

He preached the sermon "Waiting to Exhale: Robin and the Painful Past" during the "Waiting to Exhale" series.

The fiery issues of life wage war against more than just the flame of relationships, and without the help of God, many have been consumed. It is my prayer that through these encouraging messages couples will know that, if it is their prayerful desire, God is able to give courage under fire, defeat the enemy, and restore their covenant.

1

Unsung: The Story of Jacob

So the gifts were sent on ahead, while Jacob himself spent that night in the camp. During the night Jacob got up and took his two wives, his two servant wives, and his eleven sons and crossed the Jabbok River with them. After taking them to the other side, he sent over all his possessions. This left Jacob all alone in the camp, and a man came and wrestled with him until the dawn began to break. When the man saw that he would not win the match, he touched Jacob's hip and wrenched it out of its socket. Then the man said, "Let me go, for the dawn is breaking!" But Jacob said, "I will not let you go unless you bless me." "What is your name?" the man asked. He replied, "Jacob." "Your name will no longer be Jacob," the man told him. "From now on you will be called Israel, because you have fought with God and with men and have won." "Please tell me your name," Jacob said. "Why do you want to know my name?" the man replied. Then he blessed Jacob there. Jacob named the place Peniel (which means "face of God"), for he said, "I have seen God face to face, yet my life has been spared" (Genesis 32:21-30, NLT).

Television in America . . . it has hit rock bottom, hasn't it? Though I won't go into all of my normal treatment of the decline of TV, suffice it to say that I trace the most detrimental moments to the creation and subsequent explosion of reality shows in America. This is the only country where reality shows work like they do and the following fictional reality show narrative would even be possible. America is the only place that:

In this *Amazing Race* called life, while many of us seek to be an *American Idol* and move from being an *Apprentice* to earning and owning, we feel it behooves us to be more than a *Bachelor* or *Bachelorette*; no matter what *Big Brother* says. So we might go on a *Blind Date* only to find out that we are the *Biggest Loser*, which leads to one of us ending up on *Cheaters* thinking, "I could have been a *Contender* on *Danger Island*." However, instead we opt for an *Extreme Makeover* to overcome our *Fear Factor* of those who have been *Growing Up Gotti* or at least lived there as a *Houseguest*.

Until you realize, "*I Hate My Job*" and long to meet *Joe Millionaire* or at least the *Average Joe*. But now you know that is a joke and you sound like *The Last Comic Standing* while your friends are busy with the *Making of Their Band*. Unfortunately your daydream is interrupted by your *Big Fat Obnoxious Boss* who makes you work late so you have to call your *Nanny 911* who is over the *Osborne's* house waiting for *Xzibit's Pimp My Ride*. When it doesn't happen, they realize that they've just been *Punk'd* by the boys from *Queer Eye for the Straight Guy*. Now back to the *Real World*, where the *Sports Illustrated Swimsuit Model Search* has a few men thinking about *Trading Spouses*; or at least is providing them temptations that prove to be the *Ultimate Love Test*. Since your money is not where you want it to be, you are the one *Who Wants to Be a Millionaire* or definitely the one *Who Wants to Marry a Millionaire*.

2

> Right now your pocket is looking like *The Weakest Link*, and it makes you want to treat your bill collectors like *WWF Monday Night Smackdown*, but you can't do that because that is not reality, especially when you realize that now you can win *America's Got Talent* with no talent and be one of *The Real Housewives of Atlanta* without having a house or a husband.

It has, indeed hit rock bottom hasn't it? However, there is one saving grace in the genre of non-reality reality television and that is the offering by TV One called *Unsung*. It presents past and current stars and celebrities from music, television and cinema that for whatever reason, just before or just after their success ran into difficulty, fell from grace, and consequently caused their career to be looked at as unsung.

One night, while watching this brilliant show, I began to wonder what it would look like if it featured the life of biblical celebrities. As I did this, my mind began to peruse the pictorial of biblical characters, both big and small, that matched the rudimentary and routine-like mold of *Unsung*. I caught a sensory snag on the life of Jacob and I began to imagine what an *Unsung* show of Jacob's life would be like. That is when my version of the show came on: UNCOMPROMISED, UNRECOGNIZED, AND UNPARALLELED . . . Unsung: The Story of Jacob.

As the show opened, I saw Jacob standing at a microphone in front of a crowd of people and as he approached it, I noticed that his walk was very deliberate and intentional but definitely disturbed. He tapped the mike and said, "Testing! Testing!" Then he said words that might be familiar to some but I admit they threw me off. He said, "My name is Jacob and I am an addict." The people said, "Hi, Jacob!" He smiled, took a deep breath, and said, "I'm sure some of you are thrown off by my confession, but there are two reasons that you have never heard of this part of me. In fact, it is not even in the record of my story in the Bible. I'll tell you one reason now and save one 'til the end. The initial reason is that this is the first time I have ever felt comfortable sharing my story."

Before he could finish the whole story, my mind began to rehearse the Sunday school lessons of Jacob's life. As I began to do so, I wondered if I could have ever seen this coming. Revelation came as I familiarized myself with the study of addictive behaviors, causes, symptoms, and triggers. It was then that I saw that this confession in my version of *Unsung* was way more than possible, more than plausible, and more likely probable; that if Jacob's *Unsung* episode did not include his addiction, it definitely would have included his addictive behavior.

You see, addiction or addictive behavior is generically defined as the cause of one who becomes physiologically or psychologically dependent on a substance such as alcohol or a narcotic. However, I hated that particular definition because it seemingly pigeonholed a small group while letting others off the hook. But there was another wonderful definition that I believe we will use as our working definition for this offering. Addiction is when one habituates to something compulsively or obsessively, and is willing to abandon a true and normal sense of self to the point that it becomes the new normal.

It is said to be caused on several different levels from biological to psychological and even to sociological, and these are ironically seen in Jacob as well as in the lives of those of us with the strong testimony that we have been delivered. In fact, it is even in the lives of those of us who do not want to admit it. Because the qualifying reasoning for addictive behavior is the excessive, repetitive use of pleasurable activities to cope with unmanageable internal conflict, pressure, and stress; all of us, if we are truthful, whether we like or not, are guilty of some type of addictive behavior—behavior that in a real sense reveals to us that we can be addicted to more than just crack, heroin, cocaine, meth, prescriptions, and alcohol. It is so easy for some of us to point fingers, but what about the repetitive use of other things that, if we don't have them, it will mess with our psychological and physiological realities? I mean, what about the addictive behaviors we have concerning food, work, exercise, gambling, sex, porn, shopping, Facebook and social media, Starbucks, reality shows, cell phones, gossip, co-dependency, and yes, even church. The truth is that when we don't get a hit of these things we will act in ways that are not normal to us and change ourselves into something that becomes the new normal.

As I tuned back into the show, I heard Jacob say what was the most crazy. He suggested that there is pressure put on those of us who could potentially be addicts because we are the most gifted. We are the ones who have charisma, the ones who have intelligence and creativity. We are the ones who long to be honest and whom people expect to lead. But gifts come with burdens, like low self-esteem and the feeling of being inadequate. I mean, what does it mean to and for me that when you say I'm great, I don't believe it? It comes with stress and the impulsivity of trying to prove myself and the desire to get ahead and prove to myself and others that I am of worth.

That is when, in my version of *Unsung*, Jacob began to tear up and said, "All of my life I have been fighting to be good enough. Even in my mother Rebekah's womb, I was in a fight with my twin brother, Esau, for nourishment, for food, and to be first. We fought so hard that my mom had complications. I was just trying to be good enough, but Esau was born first. As a result, even though God told my mother that Esau would one day serve me, I was born a loser."

"If that was not enough, while growing up my father, Isaac, liked Esau better than he liked me. I couldn't help that Esau was stronger, had more hair, and was tougher. I had allergies and I did not like hunting, but you remember my dad was an outdoorsman like his dad, Granddaddy Abraham. Not me, I was softer and more timid. In fact, rather than going outside, I liked being in the kitchen with mama. So you know they bullied me at school, called me bad names and questioned my sexuality and my machismo. However, that didn't hurt as bad as the disappointment in my dad, Isaac's, eyes when he looked at me. It was different than how he looked at Esau, and though I already felt like a loser, now I feel like a letdown."

"So I decided to cope and feel good the best way that I could. I decided that I was going to live up to my name. My name means supplanter or trickster, and that is one thing I was good at. In fact, I didn't even have to wait long before prime opportunity would arise. One day I was cooking some stew and Esau returned home from a long hunt. He was hungry and wanted some stew. I told him he would have to sell me his birthright if he wanted some of this stew. Reluctantly he did it and I got his birthright for stew. That was my thing. I could get over on people. I don't know why I was so good; I just was. At the height of every addiction develops the ability to get over on people, no matter the cost to the relationships. It was just natural to me and I didn't know why, until . . ."

"That morning my mother called me to her and said that she had just overheard my father preparing and planning to give Esau the blessing. She looked at me and devised a plan that we were going to trick my father and steal Esau's blessing. I didn't realize it then, but now I do, that it was at that moment that I should have seen that the addictive behavior that we struggle with is often generational. My mother was a trickster! She is the one who told and taught me how to trick my father and steal the blessing, the mantle, and the substance of my father before he died. She had it planned down to the very last details: the recipe of the lamb, the wool on my arms, the robe for the blessing, and even how to disguise my voice."

"And I did it; I stole the blessing, and when Esau heard he vowed to kill me. So my mother had a contingency plan for me to run.

That too, of course, is the sign of addictive behavior—the lack of ability to take responsibility for the mess that one has made. I admit I was scared and I ran just like my momma said to go to my Uncle Laban's house, and when I got there I found out he was a trickster too. I'm not going to lie, Uncle Laban got me a couple of times, but ultimately I tricked him and used his own resources to become richer than he."

"Now some time has passed, but I am OK. I am stronger, wiser, and better. I am twice married, not because I divorced but because I have two wives. Things are going well, I am successful, and I am just about to go to the land of Canaan, which was the land of my grandfather, the land of the promise. But before I can get to the promise I hear that Esau, whom I have not seen in about 20 years, is not only looking for me but is on his way to me. BOOM! That is when a daunting reality hit me that God loves us so much that most times, before he allows us to walk into the promises of the future, God makes us face the unresolved issues of our past in our present."

"There I am on the precipice of my promise and God makes me face my past. So once again, like the hustler I am, I tried to get around it. After I sent the gifts across the Jabbock River and I tried to lie down to slumber, I could not sleep. After pacing for a while, I sent both my wives, Leah and Rachel, across into the Promised Land with my children and my servants while I remained on the other side. I stayed because I still had issues from the past to deal with."

"That's when the deepest, darkest moment of my life hit me, and I dare to believe that this moment happens in the life of anyone who has ever struggled with any type of an addiction. This is the darkest point of addiction and that is that when you get close to your promise but have to stand by yourself, with yourself, and confront yourself. All of your excuses are gone and you cannot blame anyone. You cannot cute your way out, drink or smoke your way out, sex or porn your way out, spend or network your way out; you have to confront yourself, by yourself, with yourself. For me this was too much, as I was already too stressed out. My family is in the Promised Land and I'm hoping that they are safe. I have to deal with my brother tomorrow, a brother whom I have not seen in 20 years, and the last time I saw him I stole his patriarchal blessing. Now I am by myself, facing myself with myself. All of this should have been enough, but then it happened. . . . Somebody hit me! Somebody picked a fight with me!"

"I knew it had to be Esau sneaking up on me like he used to when we were young. He used to beat me up all of the time, but not today. In the words of the *YouTube* sensation Sweet Brown, "Ain't nobody got time for that!" So we are fighting and we are going at it; I was determined not to lose to Esau this time. I was wrong for stealing his stuff and getting over on everyone, but I just did not want to be the loser again. We fought so intensely that it was almost morning and the sun was about to rise. It was when this dude saw that he could not beat me that he hit me in my hipbone and dislocated my hip. Of course now I was injured, but I kept fighting; I was broken but I still had some fight in me."

"Then the man said, 'Let me go!' When I heard his voice I knew it wasn't Esau. I thought to myself, 'Really? You picked the fight with me. I was minding my own business, dealing with the potential consequences of my own addictive behaviors; then I end up fighting you, just defending myself, and you injure me. Now you demand that I let you go?' I thought all of that but only one statement came out. I said, 'I won't let You go 'til You bless me.'"

"I thought about the fact that I have been through too much to come out of this thing empty-handed. I have suffered too much, prayed too much, and cried too much. I have lied sometimes, had to apologize sometimes. I've been running and fighting too long and too hard not to get a blessing out of this. I'm injured, I'm broken, and I wanna quit, but I can't let go. I need you now—not another second or minute but right now! Father, I stretch my hands to Thee, and if I let go, I might miss something. 'I won't let You go till You bless me!' He asked me my name and I asked him his and we had a face off."

"One more thing happened, but before I tell you that I want to say one thing. Yes, I was injured in that fight and, yes, I have this ugly limp. But don't feel sorry for me. Don't look down when you see me walking with a cane because of my limp. Don't feel bad, because my limp is not impairment but it is proof that I have seen God's face. I named the place Peniel because I have seen the face of God. Every time I limp I'm reminded of His face."

"Oh, I know why you are not shouting. You are waiting for the second reason that you had never heard about my addictions or my addictive behaviors. You are wondering how it is possible that you have been in Sunday school all of your life and heard me preach a thousand times but never knew about my addiction or addictive behaviors. The reason is because God changed my name and my record was expunged! And I wonder, is there anybody here who can touch your neighbor and say, 'You can't call me what you used to 'cause He Changed my name! Say Yeah! Yeah!'"

2

The Re-Education of Plastic Barbie

These events happened in the days of King Xerxes, who reigned over 127 provinces stretching from India to Ethiopia. At that time Xerxes ruled his empire from his royal throne at the fortress of Susa. In the third year of his reign, he gave a banquet for all his nobles and officials. He invited all the military officers of Persia and Media as well as the princes and nobles of the provinces. The celebration lasted 180 days—a tremendous display of the opulent wealth of his empire and the pomp and splendor of his majesty.

When it was all over, the king gave a banquet for all the people, from the greatest to the least, who were in the fortress of Susa. It lasted for seven days and was held in the courtyard of the palace garden. The courtyard was beautifully decorated with white cotton curtains and blue hangings, which were fastened with white linen cords and purple ribbons to silver rings embedded in marble pillars. Gold and silver couches stood on a mosaic pavement of porphyry, marble, mother-of-pearl, and other costly stones.

Drinks were served in gold goblets of many designs, and there was an abundance of royal wine, reflecting the king's generosity. By edict of the king, no limits were placed on the drinking, for the king had instructed all his palace officials to serve each man as much as he wanted.

At the same time, Queen Vashti gave a banquet for the women in the royal palace of King Xerxes.

On the seventh day of the feast, when King Xerxes was in high spirits because of the wine, he told the seven eunuchs who attended him—Mehuman, Biztha, Harbona, Bigtha, Abagtha, Zethar, and Carcas—to bring Queen Vashti to him with the royal crown on her head. He wanted the nobles and all the other men to gaze on her beauty, for she was a very beautiful woman. But when they conveyed the king's order to Queen Vashti, she refused to come. This made the king furious, and he burned with anger (Esther 1:1-12, NLT).

She was born Onika Tanya Maraj on December 8, in either 1982 or 1984 in the city of St. James on the Island paradise of Trinidad and Tobago. The date is questioned because the birth records on the Island are unclear which birth year is accurate. Raised in the early years primarily by her grandmother, she and her mother relocated to the borough of Queens, New York, to find opportunities and a fresh start in America, away from her twice-addicted and abusive father.

It was in Queens, New York, in the mid 1980s that a major revolution was taking place as Queens, along with the Boogie down Bronx, were the partners who conceived a child called hip hop. It was during this time that the embryo of this musical genre was growing and maturing. It was hip hop there in both the Bronx and in Queens that started this movement of music that kept it real, and we fell in love with it from the moment we heard *Rapper's Delight*.

Now it must be quickly noted that when hip hop was in the formation stage, its umbilical cord was tied heavily to the social ills in the community as it prophetically reported the heartbeat of the street. You remember Grand Master Flash's song, *The Message*: "Don't push me cuz I'm close to the edge I'm trying not to lose my head. . . ." This was a social justice anthem that was critiquing the unfair and downright criminal economic practice of Reagonomics and its trickle-down theory, which suggested that the wealth should be at the top and as time passed it would trickle down to the poor and when it did everyone's boat would rise. But in the words of Dr. Freddie Haynes III, pastor of Dallas mega church Friendship West Baptist, "What if you don't have a boat? In fact, what if you don't even have a car, a job, or a house? Or what if, as Africans on American soil, we are still waiting—after over 150 years—for our boat to come in?" This art form—hip hop—spoke directly to our plight.

Hip hop created a new genre and art form of music—music that was different from the norm. It did not use routine instruments but a DJ on the turntables to provide the beat and a hype man whose job it is to excite the crowd and promote the rapper. This is how Flavor Flav made his career with, "Yeah, Boyeeee!" This genre featured the MC, a storyteller in the oratorical African spirit of the griot. The griot and/or the MC act as the official storyteller of the history and the truth of a particular people; he is a street preacher of sorts who proclaims a "gospel" of the plight of the people. Although their telling of the story offers no hope of prescription that results in the healing of the people's situation, the telling of it gives hope to the people that at least now the truth is out.

This was the beginning of hip hop until it became corrupted. There on the same street, when word got to the major record executives about how much money this hip hop movement was worth and how much trouble it was stirring by having the courage to speak truth to power, a plan was put in place. This plan was to force hip hop mainstream and make it commercial. With it came wealth that before was unfathomed, but it also came with rules. If you wanted to participate in the new hip hop game you could not refer to black men as a god or a king, but now they were to be niggas, gangstas, and dogs. Our sistas were no longer to be Nubian princesses or Queens of the Nile but shorties, hoochies, bitches, hood rats, and hoes. The rules also implied that the promotion of street life was success at all cost—not the Beloved Community in which the goal was for us to come up together, but rather you get yours and I'll get mine but I bet I get mine first.

This was around 1986, and though I am not a conspiracy theorist, the timing of this change was eerily close to the time that crack cocaine hit the street, which ironically directly or indirectly not only forced hip hop and the drug game to become strange bedfellows but it also forced the social poets underground. As a result, if you were a hip hop artist with a conscience or told the truth, you could not get a deal.

This is the climate of the Queens, New York, in which Onika grew up—a place of poverty where everyone wanted to be on the come- up; an environment where one of the games—music or dope—would be the ticket to get you out. Everyone had a dream and a mix tape, a collection of their songs to sell. So it was for Onika who, after graduating from a performing arts school and subsequently getting fired from 15 jobs due to her attitude, changed her name to Niki Minaj to pursue her music career.

Now I am not going to bore you with how she got started and all of that, but suffice it to say that today she is one of the hottest stars on the planet. She was number 8 on the top earners list in 2011–2012 and currently has 15 million Twitter followers. She has all the trappings of success; however, I ask: Is the price that she paid for success worth it?

Minaj has become known for being an emblem or symbol of the promotion of sex. From her racy lyrics filled with sexual content, about which she admitted that early in her career she was competing against men and women rappers and that she wanted to go further than the men; to her entire look—the heavy and enticing makeup, the collection of high-heel stilettos, the tight and suggestive wardrobe of clothes, and of course her body—she embodies sex. I say her body because it has been rumored since she came to the scene that she had her parts augmented in order to outdo everyone else and to rise quickly to the top of the game. And rise quickly she did. However, by doing so she became the exact opposite of who the world sees in Beyoncé, who is acceptable and non-threatening enough for the President and First Lady to have at the White House. Niki Minaj is not seen as nice, she is the poster child for naughty, and the world is eating it up.

What makes this so delectable to the palate of the world? Why has the world acquired a taste for such things? I suggest that the world has fallen in love with Niki Minaj because in many ways the world sees itself in her. You see, I believe that beneath all of the glitz and the glamour there is a struggling girl from Queens who is still trying to deal with a dysfunctional past. Underneath the makeup, the heels, and all of the plastic, there is one who is just like many of us in here today, just trying to figure out who they really are. With Onika, I mean Niki, this suggestion is seemingly seen in her creation of at least 5 alter egos—5 characters that she switches to in order to escape the pain of being who she really is. One of these characters is Barbie. This is what poet Jasmine Mans critiques Minaj about, and not only Minaj but also the countless women in America of all races that run after this plastic look, which is a façade and an escape from who they really are.

You know that look: weave, weave, and more weave; high-heel everything, including sneakers; heavy makeup, asymmetrical eyebrows; bigger breasts, bigger behind, and smaller waist; and most importantly, you must appear timeless. The goal is to look like Barbie, who is over 60 and has not changed a bit. This is the look that women young, old, short, tall, slim, or heavy chase after and spend money they don't have in order to achieve.

But in order to the let the sisters off the hook a little, they don't chase after the look of Niki Minaj or other like celebrities and knowingly or unknowingly render themselves looking like a plastic Barbie coming off of the assembly line for nothing. No! They play Barbie because they are looking for Ken and because they believe that this is what Ken likes. After all, Niki Minaj seemingly is the dream of every man, and since a good man is hard to find and a woman is in competition with other ladies, many choose to dummy down so that they can Barbie up.

This is what I believe to be the brilliance of Jasmine Mans, the young poet who critiques what she sees in Niki Minaj. Minaj is one who has such platform but is using it, according to Mans, "to trade paper [or money] in order to become plastic" and influence millions of Kens and Barbies young and old to do the same. She does this in essence by encouraging the sisters to become anything he wants you to become as long as he's paying, while at the same time saying to the brothers as long as you have the money it is acceptable to expect her to be or do whatever you want. If she doesn't, it's OK, because plastic Barbies are being made every day. This is what Jasmine Mans called "The Miseducation of Barbie." Her critique spawned me to ask: Is there no help for Barbie, for Ken?

It was in my quest for an answer that the Lord took me to a scenario in the Book of Esther. Of course, Esther is a book that primarily deals with God's power to preserve his people over and against: racism—one race's use of power to rule and control the actions of another ethnicity; classism—discrimination and pigeonholing due to a disparity in socioeconomic opportunity and the distribution of wealth; and the threat of systemic genocide—the systemic annihilation of the race not in power by the one that is in power.

This is what was to happen to the Jews in the Book of Esther. As a result, the majority of the Book of Esther deals with the rise of Hadassah, an orphaned Jewish girl, to become Queen Esther, and because of her marital relationship with the king she saved her people. This is where most people will commence and conclude their preaching or teaching in this Book. However, there is a narrative that is worth noting before the story gets to Esther.

As we look at the text we are quickly teleported back to the Persian palace of King Ahasuerus (Xerxes), where an elaborate party is being thrown. The king ruled from India to Ethiopia and decided to show off his power and riches by throwing a party for the nobles of 127 provinces. By verse four we learn that this party for the nobles lasted for 180 days. That is six months of partying. In the next verse it says that the common folk were then invited and their party lasted for 7 days. It was during this time that the King showed off his riches, giving each person a unique golden cup. It is here in the midst of the King showing his opulence that the preaching shows up.

After 186 days of partying, the King's heart was merry with wine and he summoned Vashti, his queen, to present herself. Vashti was his beautiful new queen; some scholars suggest that this party was a party that they were throwing together as her first as Queen. It has also been suggested that she was a Queen that he married during his conquests to Ethiopia, and that he married her in order to solidify political relationship with that region. If this were true then that means that Vashti's skin had been kissed by nature's sun; she was Black.

It is the middle of the party as the King was drunk that, after showing all his possessions, the King tells his 7 eunuchs to summon the Queen. She was supposed to present herself wearing the crown, arguably only the crown. The Bible says he wanted her to do this because she was beautiful. However, she refused. Upon hearing this, the King was enraged, and so were all of his guests. The guests were upset because they feared that if their wives adopted the actions of the Queen they would not retain control of their own home. So they devised and executed the plan to remove her crown and take her title as Queen.

There it is! There in the midst of classism and racism, we find flat-out sexism. Sexism is the use of power by one sex to control the actions and future of another sex.

Welcome to America, the Land of the Free and the Home of the Brave; at least that is what the songs say. In America, sexism is prominent. Even though 2 out of 3 babies born in America are female, women are considered a minority. Women very rarely earn the same wage as men—sexism. Men believe that since they have a phallic symbol affixed to their anatomy, it allows them to sire children while thinking that they are better than the woman who has the very womb they need to reproduce. That's why, as Ken, we think we control the thoughts and actions of Barbie, especially if she will change who she is to the point that she forgets who she was in order to be with him.

In the church there is sexism—men who pompously deny that God anointed women to preach. Even though most of the seminary graduates are female, in some circles they are made to preach from the floor. Though most of the time their preaching is more substantive, women are treated as second-class. Can you believe that they say that woman should not preach and should not carry the word? The Bible says that the Word became flesh and dwelt among us, which means that it took a woman to get pregnant, carry, and deliver the Word, so that men would even have something to preach about— sexism.

In our homes there is sexism. It's a woman's job is to serve the man and sing background to my solo. She can have dreams as long as they support mine. I can have other lovers but she needs to keep herself only unto me or I'll shoot. She better do what I say; after all, I have the resources; I'm the king. If I say it, do it, even if it means dancing in your crown, only your crown. This sounds like the textbook from which Niki Minaj and millions of young ladies received their mis-education.

If you let me share this with you, I will be done. There is a difference between lack of education, poor education, and mis-education. Lack of education means that for whatever reason the variable needed to give proper education is non-existent, and there is no presence of education at all. Poor education means that variables needed to give proper education are limited to the point that there is only a limited presence of education. However, mis-education is in my view the most evil enterprise there is. It is when the teacher knows the truth but purposely chooses to teach a lie. But Vashti shows up to do away with mis-educations of plastic Barbie and Ken. Vashti is here to give us Re-education.

The first thing that Vashti shows us that dignity does not lie in position and/or things. In his book, *Dangerous Calling*, Paul David Tripp shares an interesting statement, which I paraphrase. He says that oftentimes we spend time finding worth and significance in things with "assigned worth" and not "inherent" worth. We seek after the things of this world and miss the things of God. My wife and I realized this to be a reality when we were in Las Vegas. She wanted a Louis Vuitton purse and I set out with $500 to buy her one. When we walked into the store in the Shops at Caesar's Palace I spotted a purse and asked how much it cost. The lady said $2,500! By the time she showed me what my $500 could purchase, we were in the wallet and keychain section. I asked my wife how the young ladies where we are from could afford such purses because we see them all of the time, and she said that those are counterfeit. I was immediately blown away by the notion that we are a people who would base our worth, our happiness, and even more sadly our self-esteem on the things that we can acquire, even if what we acquire is counterfeit.

This was not the case with Vashti. Vashti had the mentality that said, "I might not be much, but I know who I am. I'm not gonna fake it or try to play it up or down. I'm not going to try to impress you with a counterfeit persona. You might not like it, but I got to be real. In a real sense, how I see me means more to you than how you see me. I don't need status, position, possession, or compromise; I am the me God made me, and I am persuaded to believe that with God, I am enough."

Vashti teaches us that it is possible to lose the crown and yet remain a queen. Though the palace was a great place and she most likely enjoyed being the Queen, she realized her position and things did not make her—she made them. The crown is nice but it does not make me—I make it. The house, the job, the vehicle, the clothes are all nice but I make them—they don't make me. The Bible lets us know, though, something very powerful at the beginning of Chapter 2. After a while it says the King got over his anger, but he kept thinking about Queen Vashti and law that he had passed. He did not get married to Esther for some 4 and a half years later, and the insinuation is that during all of that time the King grieved the decision in his heart. Vashti no longer had the crown, but because she wouldn't sell herself she reigned in his heart. I wish I had somebody!

3

Menace to Society

When he saw Jesus from a distance, he ran and fell on his knees in front of him. He shouted at the top of his voice, "What do you want with me, Jesus, Son of the Most High God? Swear to God that you won't torture me!" For Jesus had said to him, "Come out of this man, you evil spirit!" Then Jesus asked him, "What is your name?" "My name is Legion," he replied, "for we are many" (Mark 5:6-9, NIV).

She named him Kevin, and like any mother she fell in love with him the first time she saw him. He was to be something, something different than all of the rest—especially different than his fine, smooth-talking quick walking, dead-beat 18-year old drug-dealing father. No, Kevin was to be different, and though she was only almost 17, she was determined that her boy would be the best of the rest. Yes, it would be hard, but her heart was fixed and her mind was made up that even though her boy had the 3 deadly strikes of America—poor, Black, and male—Kevin would not strike out.

However, she did not know how hard it was raising a Black man in America. She did not assess the stresses and strains that come from poorly planned moments of pleasure. She did not have an idea how much formula cost, and even with WIC and food stamps things were harder than she ever expected. That's when she began to substitute juices and sodas for formula. As a result, little Kevin became more hyperactive and became affected by the sugar highs and lows of juice and soda. Because she needed a break from the responsibility of teenage single motherhood, she would frequently engage the television as a babysitter and allow little Kevin to watch whatever he wanted, whenever he wanted.

But as he grew, Kevin, being the intelligent, strong-willed Black young male that he was, quickly deduced that any attention is better than no attention at all. You see, it is attention and nurturing from your mother in the formative years that forge and form the seeds of self-identity. Of course, Kevin did not understand this. All he knew is that he liked attention, and if he didn't get it he would get mad. In fact, he found out that if he wanted attention all he had to do was act up. So quickly the sugar highs joined with this need for attention, and he began to pay attention only to things that got him attention.

Before long, as he began elementary school, the teachers noticed not that he could not pay attention but that in his quest for identity that he would not pay attention to anything or to anyone who would not pay attention to him. As a result they labeled him as having Attention Deficit Disorder.

If you will, allow me to park here parenthetically and tell you that I used to be an Assistant Dean at a Jr. High School in Chicago. While there I would see our boys come in diagnosed as having ADD/ADHD, and I realized that the people and system that diagnosed them have it all wrong. It is not that there is a deficit in their ability to pay attention but simply that there is a deficit in how much attention has been paid to them. In fact, I dare say . . . watch me now . . . all of us have Attention Deficit Disorder! You don't believe me? Just let the important people in your life who are supposed to be paying you attention start ignoring you, and you're going to do some things to get some attention! Let your husband or your wife quit paying the right type of attention or your parent or your child start acting funny, and your behavior will become a little suspect. All of us get to acting funny and it might seem that we have a deficit in attention, and sometimes we will even act out of character because we need and want attention.

As he grew, young Kevin craved this attention and acted out to get it. But his mother was wearying and getting tired of taking off work to go up to the school. In fact, when she was home she was so mad at him she didn't even want to look at him. She now gave him less attention. "Go outside . . . just get out of my face!" she screamed.

Kevin, now an outcast, began to kick it in the streets. He most urgently came into contact with other young brothers like him with similar beginnings and similar stories. It is these beginnings and stories that have them all in the same place at the same time, looking for self-identity and social acceptance. However, they quickly realize that this quest for identity and acceptance puts all of them in a direct competition with each other for the limited resources of attention, respect, and social acceptance. They also discover that the most-coveted place to get all of these is from pleasure with the young ladies, whom you get pleasure from by offering them possessions or stuff.

On the other side the sisters, who are struggling with their own issues, are pretty much looking for some of the same things that the boys are. They are looking for attention and things to fill the void of fatherlessness, and since the Lord has blessed her with a cute shape that gets her attention and things, she might as well give a little pleasure, especially if it gets her more things. But since respect, attention, and things that are limited, the competition rages. The young men have to outdo each other for the attention, possessions, and pleasures, and Kevin would not be outdone; he would get it at all costs; even by selling drugs, gun toting, and doing a drive-by.

He did so much and got so crazy in his pursuit of possessions, power, and pleasure that his friends gave him a nickname. It is a name that would be remembered in movie and cultural history. His nickname was O-Dog, and he was so crazy that his best friend Caine described him in the lines of the May 1993 film release, "Menace to Society," like this: "Now O-Dog is the craziest nigga alive. He is America's nightmare—young, Black, and don't give a f@*k!"

O-Dog was a menace to society caused by society. A menace, one who was thought of as threatening to America, the country who directly and indirectly has rendered the dreams of his young mother as a simple and recurring nightmare. The male fruit of her loins pigeonholed into the chasm of social catastrophe and the maze of societal dysfunction and disappointment. This country, America, has assassinated his promise, potential, and plans, and in him this produces anger, fury, and rage. He doesn't give a f@*k! It is in this rage that he refuses to chase after the process that leads to destiny and purpose. Instead he simply lives his life, in the words of Dr. Cornel West, as "a series of random nows."

Beloved of God, I must admit that I have been talking about a movie character, and furthermore I must admit that some of his early history I improvised. But when we consider the cultural clues and look at the story of O-Dog's life through the lens of the reality of the American landscape, I am sure that you will agree that O-Dog's story is not only possible but is more like probable. The historic and intentional systemic and genocidal practices of these all but United States against men of African descent on this American soil is unprecedented and unending.

The killing of Black men physically, mentally, and socially leaves young men hungry and thirsty for self-identity, living life in the series of random nows with "getting over at all costs" as their only plan. And in America, an ever-expanding consumer culture where everything and everyone has a price, with the three-headed prize of power, property, and pleasure. Young Black men are on a quest that gives them the illusion that if they get any or all of these that everything will be alright, only to find out that in this country and with the current rules you will almost always be seen as an outcast, an animal, and one worthy of disrespect. I mean, you can graduate from Harvard, become a senator of a majority white state, and even rise to the highest office in the land and someone will have the audacity to call you a lie in an open session of Congress.

It is in the depressive pseudo-reality of this that many Black men are rendered spiritually bankrupt. This eclipse of hope and absence of self-love breaks down family bonds. I mean, I can't love a wife, children, or a family if I don't love me. They have stripped me of my identity or worse yet preemptively interrupted and intercepted me from learning it. As a result I don't have faith in anything anymore. My mother's God is irrelevant to me. I have nowhere to go, so I give up and give in. Maybe they're right; maybe I am not beautifully and wonderfully made. Maybe I am not a masterpiece, a unique design by Father and Son. They're right, I should be an outcast. They just don't understand . . . Hell, I'm trying! I bet if I hurt somebody or took something they would get it. You know what, I'm just not good enough and I quit!

What is amazing is that though none of us know the young man in the story, the truth of the matter is that all of us know the young man in this story. All of us know an O-Dog in our immediate or extended family, on block, or in our neighborhood. All of us know a young brother struggling with his identity, trying to find himself, only to end up between a rock and a hard place. All of us know a brother like this; that is why it's not hard for us to identify with this young man who came running out of the tombs at Jesus and the disciples. He was naked, screaming, and had broken chains still on him.

It is the middle of a night that Jesus has just performed a miracle, and a possessed man comes from the tombs, a place where the dead lay, alone. He has broken his chains but they were still on him, and he has self-inflicted cuts on him. He has been known to make screaming sounds and shrieks in the middle of the night.

I have a question. The Bible doesn't say but I was just thinking: Where were his family and friends from the city? I mean, where are those who knew him and loved him from the city? I know that he had friends because in verse 19 of Mark 5 and in verse 39 of Luke 8, Jesus tells him to go back and tell his friends and his house. But where are they? I mean, they had to know that he was out there.

Had his family and friends given up on him? They knew he had a few problems; did they readily let him go? Did they stop sending him postcards in prison, I mean, the tombs? Maybe he embarrassed them because of his drug usage or his alcohol addiction. Maybe he was living a homosexual lifestyle or chose a girlfriend that his parents disapprove of. Speaking of parents, maybe his dad left or maybe his mother gave up on him, choosing to do her own thing. Was he abused? Maybe this person was a victim of abuse and or trapped in generational curses. Had he become his father? Did he do the thing to his kids that he hated his dad doing to him? He got no visits to the cemetery; no e-mails or text messages came to this bro. or sis. Maybe he was a soldier who had been off fighting an unjust and illegal war for invisible weapons of mass destruction, only to come back and find that the rights he fought for over there he doesn't even enjoy over here. Where are the people in the city?

He was cutting himself with stones and wearing broken chains and was known to make screaming sounds in the middle of the night. The screaming and the cutting of his own skin are called self-mortification. It shows the ultimate goal of the enemy. The ultimate goal of the enemy is not for the enemy to destroy you but it is for you to destroy yourself. I believe that he was using physical pain to ease emotional pain. I mean, he wanted to hide the pain on the inside by producing pain on the outside. He was seeking relief by self-inflicting torture. And we do it too; we run from what torments us. We eat the wrong foods when we are stressed and increase cholesterol and high blood pressure. We stay up late and drink to the point of drunkenness and sickness. We shop and spend money we don't have to ease pain. We, like the man, are cutting our own selves with stones.

But why are we screaming? We are screaming not only because seemingly there is no one to help us or even to cheer us on as we deal with our issues, but also because, like the man, we have some broken chains still on us. You see, he was no longer in bondage but he still had on shackles. This means he had broken it but he hasn't beaten it yet. Like the man, we have some stuff on us that in essence we have broken it but we ain't all the way over it. Am I by myself or is there anybody here that knows what I am talking about? There are some things in your life that you thought you were past but you had not all the way beaten it. It will leave you saying, I thought I was over it—over him, over her, over that relationship, over that job, over that grudge, over that position, over that heartbreak, over that heartache, over that disappointment, over that discouragement, over what folks thought about me—but I realize that even though I broke it, I have not beaten it. It's enough to make you scream. I need to see if there are any people who have ever gotten to a point where you just want to scream. I know that you are dressed up, but there has to be someone who ain't too deep to admit that sometimes life makes you want to scream. Why don't you let one rip: 1–2–3 Scream!!!

However, the Bible says that he was screaming in the cemetery. He was screaming in a dead place where his screaming could not even be heard. His cries for help were among those who could not help. It must be a messed-up situation to have life only to be surrounded by dead things and dead people. He was screaming amongst a people who could not hear him. No one heard him until he heard a jubilant group of fishermen coming from the sea.

The man spotted Jesus and ran and fell at his feet and worshipped him.

Now what messes me up is that nowhere in the text does it say that Jesus backed up. I believe that Jesus had compassion on this one, whom was seen as a menace to society because everything on Jesus' own résumé looked like what society would call a menace. Go with me. . . . His mother was a single teenager. Nobody had actually seen her Baby Daddy. A step daddy raised him. Before he was two, the government tried to take him out. He was raised in the ghetto called Nazareth; can anything good come from Nazareth? And he hung out with a gang called the disciples. Jesus was a menace!

Three things I see here worth shouting about. The first is that the man comes to Jesus naked. I believe that Jesus gets excited when people come to him and are not covering their stuff. In the words of the songwriter: "Just as I am without one plea but that the blood was shed for me." The second thing is that the man worshipped Jesus and he had not been delivered yet. This is a two-for-one shout! It proves that when your worship is real, Jesus will accept it with your stuff still on you. The final thing is that the man did not wait until he was delivered but he praised God in advance. Is there anybody in here who knows you don't have to wait until the battle is over? You shout right now!

4

Just a Lil Bit

When Tamar arrived at Amnon's house, she went to the place where he was lying down so he could watch her mix some dough. Then she baked his favorite dish for him. But when she set the serving tray before him, he refused to eat. "Everyone get out of here," Amnon told his servants. So they all left. Then he said to Tamar, "Now bring the food into my bedroom and feed it to me here." So Tamar took his favorite dish to him. But as she was feeding him, he grabbed her and demanded, "Come to bed with me, my darling sister." "No, my brother!" she cried. "Don't be foolish! Don't do this to me! Such wicked things aren't done in Israel. Where could I go in my shame? And you would be called one of the greatest fools in Israel. Please, just speak to the king about it, and he will let you marry me." But Amnon wouldn't listen to her, and since he was stronger than she was, he raped her. Then suddenly Amnon's love turned to hate, and he hated her even more than he had loved her. "Get out of here!" he snarled at her (2 Samuel 13:8-15, NLT).

The background for this sermon was laid a few months ago when Kirk Franklin, a brother whom I have admired for years from afar, courageously took Oprah Winfrey's stage in Chicago and admitted to having been addicted to pornography. I watched as he told the story of him going through guilt and shame. I looked in as he shared the testimony of telling his wife, who shared the stage with him. He talked of how she has been working with him and how now he has the testimony.

It was Oprah's next statement that blew my mind. She said to him, all the while this was going on you were in the church and you felt like a phony. She added, but in many cases I find that it is the church that is the real phony because they, Church people, are making the rules of what not to do but they are the main ones breaking the rules. Though Kirk could not respond fully, I want to go on record and say that in many ways I believe that Oprah was absolutely correct. I say this because it is the unfortunate reality that we don't talk about a lot of topics in church but we brag about being real.

We don't engage in fruitful conversations about divorce even though 60% of Christian couples end there. We really don't deal with teen pregnancy or adultery, and we don't talk about sexuality unless we are bashing heterosexual singles, homosexuals and lesbians. We don't honestly discuss the HIV/AIDS pandemic even though the leading demographic that is contracting the virus is African American young women. And pornography is one of the things that will make people go deaf and mute because you're not supposed to talk about stuff like that in church; just give me Jesus—that's all I need.

I must admit that I was blown away by Kirk's testimony; blown away by his candor and his courage. What would make him be so open and so honest? I believe he knew that his story is not that much different from other stories, stories that you and I know. In fact, if the statistics are true, 95% of the men who are reading this right now have immediate access to pornographic material at their home. We just don't talk about it, even though, if statistics are right, 70% of Christian men have at least a social use of pornographic material.

Let me push it further. 70% of all of the websites that are open in the world are pornographic, which is a staggering statistic when you realize that in North America there are 235M internet users. However in the church we don't talk about it. Even though our kids watch soft porn on music videos, YouTube, and Facebook every day we don't talk about it. It is one of those SSSSHHHHH topics that we much rather just manage the effects of rather than treat the disease. Even though in this country, America, the Land of the Free and the Home of the Brave, we spend more in strip clubs than we do in movie theatres, we don't talk about it. Even though media provides interest and approval in the declination of morals where the main goal is to satisfy one's appetite no matter the cost to self or others, the church refuses to talk about it. That is, until now.

The word pornography comes from the Greek word porneia. This word simply means immorality of a sexual nature/prostitute or harlot. From that etymological root we also get the word fornication, which we accept simply as meaning sex between two unmarried people; however, in the truest sense of the word, it deals with the breaking of a covenant business sex arrangement, which ends in not the selling of the whole but the bartering of parts for pleasure. In a real sense when you deal with modern-day pornography it is the fascination, the purchase, and the bartering of parts.

Walk with me a while. In a real sense this means that the person is not attracted to the whole but just to the parts. I mean the person does not want the whole, just the pieces or just a little bit. He just wants parts, not the whole. He wants an affair, not the marriage. He wants legs and thighs, not brains. He wants breasts and a behind, but not conversation. He wants the feeling of sex, not the burden of responsibility. He wants to hit it, not hang around.

I know that some of you have just turned on your "churchyness" and tuned me out by saying and thinking that I'm not close to you, but the pornographers disagree with you. You see, they market $20B a year using this part concept. All porn that is targeted to men is targeted on a part theory. They believe that if they allow you to see a little bit they will hook you to chase all the rest. They know that for the man it is a visual thing and that if they can get a man to look he will begin to slide down the slippery slope of arousal that will block anything that has to do with emotions.

We will block out wife, family, love, and tenderness because the movie's focus is not on the whole but on just a lil bit. In porn, the man is not usually interested in all of the trappings of conventional sex; he does not want foreplay and those things, he just wants to climax. The problem with this is that the body has a memory, and as a result, this is filed in the body as an acceptable and enjoyable experience, to be accessed later consciously or subconsciously. Pornographers and the media blast men all of the time to access these thoughts. They hit us with banners, commercials, and the like that accent parts. For example, since when do you have to have on a bathing suit to sell chewing gum? Men see all of these parts and they are stuck on uncontrollable overload.

Most porn shows the man dominating a subservient woman. She is doing things to him that would be distasteful at least and painful at most. But here this woman is doing it with a smile on her face and the man is filled with a hormonal and chemical overload. He, of course, has testosterone, the regular sex hormone at work, but he also is dealing with adrenaline, which brings aggression. This, coupled with the visual arousal that he sees and the physical act of masturbation that he does, produces in him a climatic moment that is 20 times more addictive than crack and 5 times more addictive than meth. This chemical arousal and overload is virtually impossible to recapture in the marital bed, and as a result usually when a man is dealing with pornography, his sex life in reality will suffer. After all, pornography is perfection. The women are flawless and perfectly proportioned. They don't come with a mortgage, monthly bills, or mouth; you don't have to deal with the whole thing, just a lil bit.

For women, pornographers market the exact opposite, because most of the time women are not just aroused by sight or what they see but by situation and how they feel. On a foundational level the romance, the flowers, and the foreplay flatter them. This is how the pornographers market to them. When they are targeting women, the people in the movie do not have to be perfect. In fact, they can be regular-looking folk. This so that the woman can put herself into the scene because women are smart enough to know that life hardly ever produces perfection.

However, because they love their men, they will fake it for their men. They will become plastic like Barbie in order to comply with the immaturity of men who are addicted to the fantasy of perfection. Why do you think that there is all of this stuff out there to help the appearance of women? You have pushups and pull downs, lift ups and hold backs, weaves and tips, colored contacts and silicon racks—all of this so that women can use stuff they don't need, to compete with women they don't know, to make their parts look better than other Barbies. By doing so they are constantly and consistently playing down the whole of who they are in order to arouse men who cannot help themselves, to men who are addicted to parts.

It is because men are addicted to parts that women will seek the fantasy of having the not-so-fantastic thing of man being romantic and loving her for her, and even though the sister wants the whole thing she will settle for just a lil bit. Even though she wants more than tall, dark, and handsome, buffed arms and chest, she will settle for it because it is seemingly all that is available. She at this point is a candidate for the affair because she wants someone, even if he is someone else's someone. She is searching for someone to compliment, court her, and converse with her, and she finds him in romance novels, in movies on *Lifetime*, or in the cubicle next to her at work.

Meanwhile it is an unhealthy cycle because women will give a lil bit of their parts for a lil bit of romance while men have been trained to give a lil bit of romance for a lil bit of the parts. It is this that takes men on a slippery slope of arousal, and because of the pop-ups that the pornographers use, men find themselves exposed to and maybe even aroused by things they never thought in a million years that they would be exposed to. This is how it starts: regular heterosexual porn that evolves into looking at transsexuals, (chicks with *icks), to looking at violent sex, to looking at children or kiddie porn. It can lead to extramarital affairs, to verbal and physical abuse, and in worst cases, to the molestation of a minor, depression, rape, and divorce. It is all started by being addicted to parts, and I think that this is what Amnon was dealing with when he saw his half-sister Tamar.

In our text, we meet King David's son Amnon. He is David's oldest and heir to the throne, and he was violently in lust with his half-sister Tamar. However, though Tamar was a virgin, Amnon wanted her and concocted a plan with his cousin to get her. He pretended to be sick and sent word to his father that he needed Tamar to come and to cook for him. When she came he made advances toward her, but she asked him to ask for her hand if he really wanted her. She said if we do this the wrong way, you will break the Law of Israel, you will do something that is beneath you, and you will bring shame to me. If you want me, take the whole thing, don't just settle for a little bit.

But he did not listen to her and he violently raped her. When he finished raping her, the Bible says that he hated her and sent her away in shame. What in the world would make him do this? I contend that though she was willing to give him everything, he just wanted a little bit. I mean, it seemingly would take too much work to deal with the whole thing; he only wanted the parts. He was infatuated with pieces of her, probably even to the point that wherever he looked he saw her. He was of age, so he probably had been with some of the concubines, but the lust for her was so strong that I suggest that she had made an imprint on his mind that led him to think of her no matter who he was with.

This is one of the dangers of pornography to conventional love-making—the fact that the mind has the ability to save, to cut, and to paste, which means that it is possible to be with one person but through fantasy have parts of another person on them. In a real sense, a man can be with his own wife or girlfriend but be seeing a model's face, a singer's legs and thighs, and an actress's hips. A man could reason: I mean, my wife does alright, but it's a lot better if I imagine that she is a professional like the girl in the movie. As a result, you are cheating on your spouse or significant other with your own spouse or significant other.

Amnon wants just a lil bit. Tamar begs him to talk with the king and marry her, but he does not listen. He takes her, and he hates her. I argue that the end result of pornography and the bartering of parts and pieces is broken relationship. You see, Amnon hated her because in the very end, after he got what he wanted, after he raped her and after he enjoyed just a lil bit, he found out what most men and women find out and it made him furious. After they have had the affairs, they find out and are furious. After the woman risks everything and becomes a mistress, or after a man enters into an adulterous affair, that's when they find out. After they have moments in pornography they find out and are angry.

What do they find out? They find out that life never allows you to sign up for just a little bit. Life never lets you just enjoy parts. No, life demands that you sign up for the whole. It is impossible to have a solid relationship at home if you give your best to someone on the Internet. It is impossible to have love at home when you gave it away at the hotel. It is impossible to have compliments at home if you gave it away at the job. It is impossible to have healthy love as a single when you spend your thoughts in unhealthy places.

Life is made up not of parts but of the whole, and this was a depressing realization for Amnon, as it should have been for Kirk or for me or for anyone else who has ever battled an addiction to pornography. For all of us who have ever wanted just a little bit and got it, the result is it's depressing and will make you angry. But the shout is that just as life doesn't offer just a little bit, the just life forces us to sign up for the whole. The shout is that this is Jesus' ministry to and for us. He never fixes us just a little bit, but He makes us whole. If any man be in Christ he is a new creature.

Jesus did not give us just a little bit; he gave all of himself. I'm told that on a hill far away there was an old rugged cross; it was a symbol of suffering and shame. As I look back over my life and think about how many bits and pieces it was in, I can say I love that old cross and I love it so much that I have decided that I'm gonna stop giving God just a little bit. I've decided that I've got to do more, give more, say more, help more, pray more, and praise more. Since He gave me all of him, I cannot give him just a little bit. I've got to give him all. So y'all, I'm running, trying to make a hundred. 99½ won't do!

5

It's Always Business; It's Never Personal

After this it came about that he loved a woman in the valley of Sorek, whose name was Delilah. The lords of the Philistines came up to her and said to her, "Entice him, and see where his great strength lies and how we may overpower him that we may bind him to afflict him. Then we will each give you eleven hundred pieces of silver. . . ."

When Delilah saw that he had told her all that was in his heart, she sent and called for the lords of the Philistines, saying, "Come up once more, for he has told me all that is in his heart." Then the lords of the Philistines came up to her and brought the money in their hands. She gave him sleep on her knees, and called for a man and had him shave off the seven locks of his hair. Then she began to afflict him, and his strength left him. She said, "The Philistines are upon you, Samson!" And he awoke from his sleep and said, "I will go out as at other times and shake myself free." But he did not know that the Lord had departed from him (Judges 16:4-5, 18-20, NASB).

This, my father said, is the tension between men and women: Men want sex and women want companionship and we are willing to barter in order to get what we want. Men will give companionship, he said, to get the sex, and women will give sex in hopes of companionship. This, of course, in many cases begins a dance of dysfunction that we see more than ever ending in divorce because of inherent flaws in the foundation of the relationship.

Think about it: Many—if not most—men at their core would spell the word "romance" with three letters: S-E-X. Men are aroused by sight and are driven by their addiction to parts. He's caught up with legs and thighs, not brains and conversation. Breasts and hind parts turn him on, not responsibility and commitment. Conversely, ladies, for the most part, are not aroused as much by sight are attracted to the situation, the romance, and the like. Their mature desire says that you don't have to be perfect, just attentive. You can even be ugly; just smell good and dress nice.

Ladies, for the most part, desire it all: intimacy, companionship, and love, even marriage. However, since all of it is not available, ladies will play down the desire for it all and begin to dish out pieces of herself so that she can compete with the other ladies to get a man or at least her share of a man. Of course while this woman is grudgingly giving her pieces away she notices that there are many would-be takers: many men who are interested in a woman who would give away parts and not ask them to consider the whole. As a result she devises a plan that will qualify who is worthy of her pieces and parts.

What, you might ask, is this brilliant plan that will determine who can have her? What system has she devised to prove the worthiness of her suitors? Gold digging!

Yes. She starts the business of gold digging. She says to herself, *If all I am is pieces and if all you want is parts, at least let me get paid for it.* She thinks to herself, *I don't like it, but if I have to give up my dreams of a husband, two kids, and a dog for a share of your man while you are at work, at least let me get my light bill paid.* She thinks to her part-time boyfriend, *If you are going to leave me too like the others have, at least leave me something on the night-stand other than a condom wrapper.* She thinks to herself, *If I am going to just give the parts while others get the whole, at least let me get some gold. Even though I know that there is nothing worth what I am giving up, at least with the gold I can attempt to fill the emptiness I feel afterwards. The gold will help me feel not as bad, as broken, and as cheap.*

She goes after the gold and she becomes a gold digger. Selling herself as she seeks to anesthetize the pain with Gucci, Prada, and Louis Vuitton. Turning favors so that she might eat Filet Mignon and Lobster or have an Appletini here or a Long Island there. She may even have a good time to get her car note paid or so the kids can have some diapers. Let me push it further. She maybe will let Mrs. So and So's Mr. come by the house so that her rent will be paid. Or she will have friendships where he will do some work around the house and she blesses him with her body. Or maybe like the hit song by Kanye West suggests, because he's a pro athlete and makes money she decides that he would be a good baby daddy, even though like in the song she knows that the baby is not his. But it's cool because even though this is not what she wanted to sign up for—she'd much rather have the white house and the fence—if this is the best it can be she might as well do it well and be paid well for it. She goes for the gold; she has become a gold digger.

I know you think that I am about to drop the text on you because hermeneutically and homiletically it would be a wonderful place to do so. After all of that wonderful intro it would be almost pure genius to now take you to the text and concretely solidify my point by telling you that Delilah was the Queen of all gold diggers. But I cannot do that because so far this treatment is sounding too heavy on the women and my desire is for all of us to see this—men, women, boys, and girls. So let's use this as a workable definition for a gold digger: A gold digger is anyone who is committed to secretly advancing his or her efforts and interests toward a goal by using the relationship and resources of another. This means that if I am trying to get ahead but you have what I need and I commit myself to use you to get where I need to go, then I'm a gold digger.

You see, when we broaden what the gold is and posit that the gold is anything of worth that you are willing to use someone else to get, we are hit with the shocking reality that in some shape or form all of us have been or are gold diggers. Yes, we gold dig! We dig for the gold of material things, the gold of social standing, and the gold of economic position. We gold dig for career-related things. We gold dig for relational things. We even gold dig for physical pleasures. When we broaden the definition of gold we find that all of us have been gold diggers. Please know that I did not say that to offend you, because I understand why we do—after all, gold digging is the American way. In fact, it is the way of the world. I will allow you to obtain what I don't have, then I will scheme and come up with a plan to use you to take it from you.

Is this not the Eurocentric way of thinking? It's isolated and all about me. It is the antithesis to the African way of thinking, where, as John Mbiti said, identity is formed within the group and success is a community event. No, I'd much rather sit back and watch you obtain and achieve the gold, and then I will come and dig your gold. It's European and its anti-community.

This way of thinking prevails in this country, is seen in the media, and is even taught in our schools. How in the world did Christopher Columbus "discover" America when there where people here when he got here? Gold digging! During slavery white men came to the West coast of Africa, looking for cheap labor. They found hues of chocolate, brown, and caramel on the backs of men and women, our foreparents who built this country. When they took us they were gold digging! They gave us the worst of the worst, but we made it. They didn't give us ham and bacon, but they gave us hog parts. We took the parts and made hog headcheese, ate pig feet, and turned chitlins into a delicacy. They took the ideas and formed processing companies to sell Chitterlings, and when they took our ideas they were gold digging.

It is the same thing that they do with sports; most of the rosters in almost every sport are full of us, yet there are not that many of us in the front office. They are gold digging. When we look at rap music and the hip hop culture, they sell our language, our dress, and our style, yet still do not give us an equal footing in the economics of the business. This country is chock full of gold diggers. It makes sense, though, doesn't it? Especially when the former President himself was a gold digger. Any time you let thousands of Americans soldiers continue to risk their lives while you secure the liquid gold called oil beneath the ground—the same ground that has been soaked by the blood of both American and Iraqi boys— President Bush was a gold digger!

If I have not got you yet, let me tell you about the biggest gold diggers. These are they who come into church week after week, sit up the seats, look up the lights, and soak up the heat but never put nothing back. They don't praise, don't shout, don't worship, don't give, but they have the audacity to critique the choir and diss the deacons. These are they who will get close to the minister of music to get a song and close to the pastor or his wife to get a hook up or a job reference. They will pay tithes twice just so they can request financial help. It's called gold digging.

When we really look at gold digging for what it really is, we find out that all of us, like Delilah, either are or have been gold diggers. You know her story. For forty years the Philistines were oppressing the Israelites; however, God raised up a judge to deliver them from their oppression. His name was Samson. Even though he was anointed as a child to be a Nazarite and though he was a priest, Samson had a thing for seedy women. Worse yet he could not shake his obsession for Philistine women. I don't think that Samson was struggling with a lust for parts, because his story tells us he was looking for a good solid relationship. In fact, in the 14th chapter he falls in love and wants to do right, but because of the racial and religious differences between him and his wife, the Philistine men question her loyalty and she sells him out. But because of his love for her, he took her back.

After the reconciliation, her people kill both her and her father. Samson gets revenge on them and the Bible says that he kills 1,000 of their men with a jawbone of an ass. However, even though he got revenge, he was still empty. Even though he made them pay he still bore the pain, and even though they were supposedly even he still did not have any joy. As a result of this emptiness he travels to Gaza and somehow ends up in the red light district. That's when he sees her walking down the popular stroll, and the Bible says he takes her. He just lost his wife, he sleeps with a prostitute, and now he is surrounded by the enemy. Someone saw him go into the house of ill repute, and now the Philistines are out there waiting for him until the morning.

The record is that at midnight Samson leaves and sneaks past all of the Philistines, but before he leaves the city he tears off the city gates and carries them away. He heads southeast to the Valley of Sorek, and before long he fell in love with yet another woman, a Philistine woman named Delilah. Though she knew that Samson loved her, Delilah did not love him. In fact, it was a set up from the very beginning. She was told to entice him, lead him on, and make him think one thing while secretly learning where his strength lies. If you do this, they say, each of us will pay you 1,100 hundred pieces of silver, and she agrees.

The record is that after a few tricks Samson finally told her his heart and, when she realized that he had given her all of him, she cashed in, tormented him and turned him over. Can't you hear Samson as he is being tied up and taken away? "Delilah, how could you do this to me? How could you play me like this? I loved you and gave you the best of me and the best I had." Can't you see

his tears and hear his heart, while she is looking, while she is count-
ing her money? If you listen closely you will hear her say, "It's
always business; it's never personal."

How did she get this way? What made her so hard? How did she
become a gold digger? How could she hurt him like that? Let's
bring it closer . . . how did you get to the way you are, where you
do not care about how much work they went through to get
there—you just want to use them to get what you want? Could it
be because you have been used and hurt? Could it be because they
left you and you are scared to be close to anybody else? Is it because
your daddy left that you don't trust men, so you gold dig your own
husband and won't trust him? You are mad at your mother, so you
treat all women like they are second-class, and because you pay
they need to do whatever you say? And if not, you will show her
with your hands who has the power?

How could you hurt her like that? How could you do that to
him? I think I know. I think I have figured it out. I think I know
why it is done. The reason is in the mentality of a gold digger. You
see, a gold digger is loyal to nothing but the gold. Delilah could not
let herself love Samson even though he was cool, well built, and
good-looking. She could never let it get too personal because she
would lose her gold-digger card. For a gold digger it's always business; it's never personal. That is the problem with many relationships today: it's always business and never personal. We are married but it is not personal; we're friends but be clear, it's business.
It's because we are scared to be vulnerable; we fear taking the
chance to be intimate.

So you had better watch your back and I will watch my back,
because it's always business and it's never personal. I will cut you
and not think about it; after all, it was not personal—only business. I can sleep with whomever I want—only business. I can cuss
out whomever—only business. I can lie, cheat, and steal—it's only
business. In fact, I can gold dig you because it's always business and

it's never personal. The two—business and personal—don't mix. That's life, isn't it? It is messed up. Everybody for themselves. It's depressing when you think of life and relationships being always business and never personal. But don't leave out God, because we serve a God who saw the condition of the world. When God saw the sinful state that mankind was in, when God realized that mankind had messed up, the Lord realized that we needed to be saved from ourselves. God pondered what to do and thought of someone to send. God sent the law and it didn't work, and God sent the judges and they failed. God sent the prophets and they could not do it, and God realized that no one could do it. Only Godself could handle the business of saving. God decided to get down to business and sent Jesus, God's only begotten Son. And that is something worth shouting about, that when God gets down to business it's never just about business—God makes it personal. Hallelujah!

6

Desperate Housewives, and the Men Who Make Them Desperate

And the rib that the Lord God had taken from the man he made into a woman and brought her to the man. Then the man said, "This at last is bone of my bones and flesh of my flesh; this one shall be called Woman, for out of Man this one was taken." Therefore a man leaves his father and his mother and clings to his wife, and they become one flesh. And the man and his wife were both naked, and were not ashamed.

Now the serpent was craftier than any other wild animal that the Lord God had made. He said to the woman, "Did God say, 'You shall not eat from any tree in the garden'?" The woman said to the serpent, "We may eat of the fruit of the trees in the garden; but God said, 'You shall not eat of the fruit of the tree that is in the middle of the garden, nor shall you touch it, or you shall die.' But the serpent said to the woman, "You will not die; for God knows that when you eat of it your eyes will be opened, and you will be like God, knowing good and evil." So when the woman saw that the tree was good for food, and that it was a delight to the eyes, and that the tree was to be desired to make one wise, she took of its fruit and ate; and she also gave some to her husband, who was with her, and he ate. Then the eyes of both were opened, and they knew that they were naked; and they sewed fig leaves together and made loincloths for themselves.

They heard the sound of the Lord God walking in the garden at the time of the evening breeze, and the man and his wife hid themselves from the presence of the Lord God among the trees of the garden. But the Lord God called to the man, and said to him, "Where are you?" He said, "I heard the sound of you in the garden, and I was afraid, because I was naked; and I hid myself." He said, "Who told you that you were naked? Have you eaten from the tree of which I commanded you not to eat?" The man said, "The woman whom you gave to be with me, she gave me fruit from the tree, and I ate" (Genesis 2:22–3:12, NRSV).

He could hardly contain himself because today was finally the day. Who would have thought that he would be this excited? He had thought he was doing fine by himself, but for some unknown reason he realized that there was something missing. It was as he moved about his neighborhood and his workplace that he noticed that seemingly everyone else had someone and everyone was happy. Though he was literally in paradise he found it not good to be alone.

God, seeing his state, decided to surprise him by causing a deep sleep to come upon him. With the hands of a Divine surgeon, the Lord took a piece of him and created someone for him. Here he is now having awakened from the slumber, waiting to see this creation; he could hardly contain himself because today was finally the day.

This narrative in many ways describes the day that many of us have experienced and others of us anticipate. For the married men in here, you remember standing at the altar, most with sweaty palms and butterflies in tow, some of us still with a hangover from the festivities of the night before. We have experienced a narrative such as this. Others of us who have not yet waded into the marital waters anticipate such a day; a day when you will stand before God and proclaim to your special one, in front of others, vows of heart and soul. It is the thing that prayers and dreams are made of, and today is the day for him.

He was not looking for just parts or just a little bit, nor was he looking for a gold-digger to secretly advance her motives and interests by using his resources. No, he was looking for a God-sent intimacy, someone to compliment and complete him, and finally his wait was over. By the way, his name is Adam, and we have a front row seat as God brings him his bride, Eve. There she is and he cannot believe his eyes.

In fact, the Bible says in verse 23 that Adam was so overjoyed with seeing her that he proclaimed, "This is bone of my bone and flesh of my flesh. She shall be called woman, for she was taken out of man." This is regularly called and considered the first wedding, the moment that marriage is instituted by the Lord himself as the first human institution. It is here that the Bible declares that man shall leave his father and mother and cleave to his wife and the two become one flesh. This means that the man and woman do not cease being individuals but they are now one, independent yet interdependent.

Independent yet interdependent means that though we are married to each other both of us should be able to hold on to who we are. It means that if either one of us has to give up who we are and what we like to have the other, but they hold on to who they are or what they like, then we are on a crash course with desperation. Because in a real sense we both should have given ourselves to each other for commitment, companionship, and covering. Neither one of us signed up to spend the rest of our lives playing in the background while the other chases dreams, aspirations, and accomplishments. I did not sign up for two becoming one and a possible;

no, I signed up for what the Bible says in verse 24, that the two shall become one and they were both naked and not ashamed.

They are in paradise and it is called the Garden of Eden. They want for nothing. We know that Adam has a job because verse 15 tells us that God had him tend and keep the garden. He also worked part-time as the namer of all of the animals. The Bible says the Lord noticed that it was not good for him to be alone and the Lord brought him someone, Eve. They get married and not only that, they both are naked but neither of them is ashamed. The deep thing about this is their nakedness. You see, when we hear the word naked, fear is automatically accessed in our psyche because most of us think of a physical nakedness. We fear being naked. We fear being that vulnerable, especially with people we don't know.

However this is not talking about being physically naked. You see, this uncovers the Divine intimacy of true relationship. It allows one to be naked and not ashamed. This type of intimacy suggests that you can uncover your spirit and not be ashamed. You can bare your emotions and not be fearful of being judged. You are able to show your fears and your dreams and not have to cover up. You can reveal who you are and not be ashamed. The reason you don't have to be ashamed is because the Lord has given you someone who will be daring enough to bare all with you. This was an awesome attribute about this husband and this wife in the text; both of them were naked but neither was ashamed.

This is a far cry from most of our relationships, isn't it? In fact, we want to show the least amount as possible. We don't want to uncover; we don't want to risk being vulnerable. We hide from our own spouses; we hide from the ones we say we love. The reason we hide is because though we can be naked physically with them we are scared to expose the real stuff. I dare say that if physical intimacy is easier for you than spiritual and emotional intimacy, then your relationship is part driven and whole deprived.

At the end of the 2nd chapter they were naked and not ashamed. However, by the second part of the first verse of the next chapter, we find that there is trouble in paradise. You see, as we focus on the narrative we notice that the woman, Mrs. Adam if you will, Sister Eve is conversing with Satan in the form of a serpent. Now I love the Bible for what the Bible does say but I also thank the Bible for the creative liberty it allows us to have. We know that Adam is not around. . . . I have a question: Where is he? Maybe he is at work or out with the boys? But what has he done that would make his wife who's at home desperate enough to be sitting here talking with a serpent, the enemy. What has he done to make her such a desperate housewife? There was trouble in paradise!

What did he do to make her lower her standards? What did he do to make her feel so insecure? What would make her feel like she has to go through his personal belongings? Why is she going through his cell phone and checking his text messages, checking financial records, or calling friends to verify whereabouts? How did she end up in these bushes trying to catch him in a lie? Why would she question her own children to find out where he took them? What would make her do this? What did Adam do? What did Adam not do? What would make Eve talk to the serpent? How did she become a desperate housewife? Indeed, there was trouble in the Garden.

Maybe Adam had some abnormal behavior. Maybe he broke his normal routine.

Maybe he is coming home late or leaving home early. It could have been that Eve had that prophetic unction that is common among the female species of African Americans—it's called women's intuition. Maybe she had caught him in some former lies. Could Adam have had some questionable plutonic relationships? Maybe he had some foul text messages or emails. Maybe he has been operating in secrecy. Maybe she felt this way because of a lack of attention and the fact that Adam won't give her any quality time.

Did he make her feel lonely? Did he make her feel powerless? I mean, she is desperate, but how did she get here?

Well, we know he did not effectively communicate with her. Look at the text when the serpent questioned her about what God said—she misquoted the Lord. Look at verse 16: Adam and the Lord are by themselves in the garden and they are having a conversation. God says to Adam, "You can have all that you want and eat of any tree, but you cannot eat of the tree of Knowledge." Fast-forward to what Eve told the serpent. She said that God said not only can we not eat it, God said that we couldn't even touch it. God did not say that. God gave the word to Adam, however the word was not effectively communicated to Eve. Is this what made her desperate?

This is not definitive, so let us keep looking. Here she is speaking with the serpent by herself, not really knowing what the Lord said. Here she is without covering, her man not with her, no effective communication from him, and the enemy is starting to make sense while he is offering her the fruit. As a result she takes it and eats it and nothing happens. She enjoyed it and offered it to her husband and he ate it; however, when he ate it something was different. When he ate it their eyes where opened and they knew that they were naked. They immediately covered themselves.

They were with the same person but all of a sudden they were embarrassed in each other's presence. They had been dating intimately for two years but now they are ashamed. They have been married for 20 years but now the intimacy is gone. They are in the same situation but now they are hiding from each other. Can't you see them arguing, their words making the situation more desperate. Don't you hear their conversations that have now turned to accusations? They are now blaming each other instead of blessing each other. They are keeping a record of their deeds, like who washed dishes or who paid the last bill. Every time they argue she loses and it makes her more desperate.

When women argue, they argue emotions and not facts. However, when men argue, they argue facts and not emotions. Furthermore, since men don't like to argue or the facts do not usually weigh in their favor, their goal is to force the women to get emotional, because men know that once women get emotional, cry, and get loud, then men will say, "See there you go, I can't talk to you, you are so insecure." And then the man will walk out.

This might have happened with Adam and Eve. The Bible doesn't say, but I was thinking it might have happened, and Eve is crying and Adam is ready to leave but they hear the Lord walking through the garden. As God is walking through, he says something that blows my mind. He says, "Adam, where are you?" Don't miss this: God holds man responsible for this turn of events. Notice that he doesn't say anything to Eve. He doesn't ask where Eve is; he wants to know where Adam is. After all, it was not sin when Eve ate the fruit. In fact, the Bible says later in 2 Corinthians 11:3 that she was deceived. However, when Adam did it the Bible says that both of their eyes were opened. God wasn't looking for Eve; he holds Adam responsible. God says, "Adam, where are you?"

Adam emerges from the bushes and says—please don't miss this—"I heard your voice; I was scared because I was naked and I hid." It is my belief that as God looks at the desperate daughters of Eve in this church, this community, this nation, and this world, God continues to ask, "Adam, where are you?" When you look at the fact that 82% of the children in Memphis City Schools are being raised by a single parent, Adam, where are you? When both married and single women are desperately fighting loneliness, and there are more men in prison than in college, Adam, where are you? The most unfortunate reality is that the resounding sound that is extracted from the actions of our men sings in concert with the words of Adam's answer: I was scared; I was exposed and I hid.

God asks, "Who told you that you were naked?" Adam said, "This woman you gave me." Adam blamed the woman and then he blamed the Lord. "This woman you gave me." He blamed her for a dysfunction that was his. There it is! This is the thing that makes ladies, women, and housewives desperate. What makes them desperate is that the men won't stand for their women; we would rather blame them than bless them. Both of them were naked, both of them were exposed, both were at risk, but he blames. The reality is that both of them have issues, the affair hurt both, both could have moved on, both could have found someone else, but he blames. Both go through the bankruptcy and save face with the children, but he blames her, and this is enough to make some desperate. When any of us are seen not as a companion but as a competitor it will make you desperate.

When she heard that he would not cover her and he blamed her, she must have been hurt and wanted to leave. He was probably ready to leave her alone. Isn't that what most brothers do when they don't want to face the facts? I know they wanted to get rid of each other, but the problem was that they were both still naked. They were both still uncovered, they were still exposed, and both were still at risk. They could not move on when both of them were exposed. They could not move forward with both of them naked. They are seemingly stuck where they are and seemingly in a situation from which they cannot get out. But stop the press. The Bible says in verse 21 that the Lord covered them. You know they had already made coverings with leaves, but the Bible says that the Lord covered them. In fact, it says that the Lord made them tunics of skins. There is the moment that desperation is quenched. That is the moment when the void of nakedness is filled. The Lord made a covering of skins. And if the Lord covered them with skins, then that means something had to die and some blood was shed.

7

Baby Mama Drama

There was a certain man of Ramathaim, a Zuphite from the hill country of Ephraim, whose name was Elkanah son of Jeroham son of Elihu son of Tohu son of Zuph, an Ephraimite. He had two wives; the name of the one was Hannah, and the name of the other Peninnah. Peninnah had children, but Hannah had no children.

Now this man used to go up year by year from his town to worship and to sacrifice to the Lord of hosts at Shiloh, where the two sons of Eli, Hophni and Phinehas, were priests of the Lord. On the day when Elkanah sacrificed, he would give portions to his wife Peninnah and to all her sons and daughters; but to Hannah he gave a double portion, because he loved her, though the Lord had closed her womb. Her rival used to provoke her severely, to irritate her, because the Lord had closed her womb. So it went on year by year; as often as she went up to the house of the Lord, she used to provoke her. Therefore Hannah wept and would not eat. Her husband Elkanah said to her, "Hannah, why do you weep? Why do you not eat? Why is your heart sad? Am I not more to you than ten sons?" (1 Samuel 1:1-8, NRSV)

It was that time of year again, and she could already feel herself getting sick. Don't get me wrong, for the most part everything was fine; I mean, her man loved her and she was desperately in love with him. She was married to Elkanah, and he was of the priestly line of the Levites, a grandson of Korah. He was favored. He would be similar to the one who had the football scholarship and won the Heisman Trophy. He played in the pros for about ten years only to tear his ACL in the Pro Bowl. Or he was that straight-A student that graduated from Morehouse and Harvard. Whatever the case, it was a great thing that he invested his money so well and that he could give her everything she wanted.

You know, their house was very nice; they lived in the mountains of Ephraim, about nine miles North of Jerusalem, and everyone knows that the hills have the best real estate with panoramic views. In fact, you probably even saw her house on *MTV Cribs*. She drove the tightest of cars—a new whip for every day of the week. However, though she wore the best, though she smelled the best, and though she had the best, it was that time of year again, and she could already feel herself getting sick.

I mean, why couldn't it be like it used to be? Man, she could remember the good old days, when it was just him and her, when they were the only two in the house, just the two of them in love, when the dinner tab had only two drinks and only two entrees. That was when this annual trip was fun and she could still remember how great it was. She was on his arm and she loved it, but more than that she loved that he loved it too. She loved the way he was proud to show her off. He'd say, "Hey everybody, this is Hannah. Ain't she fine?" Though she was embarrassed, those were the words that would melt her heart.

But that was then, before they found out that though he gave her everything she wanted there was one thing that she could not give him. That was before; before they found out that they could not have kids, before the doctors told her that she could not conceive. That was before, when she felt as if she was the apple of his eye. That was then, when she was the only one, but this is now, after he has married another woman to bear his children. Peninnah is her name. This is now, after Peninnah has had several children, children that she, Hannah, should have born. I mean, how could God do this to her? After all her name means the grace and mercy of God, and she probably felt grace and mercy back then; but this is now, when she feels no grace and feels no mercy.

This is now, after this woman has shown off her multiple baby bumps, had multiple children, and now she and the kids are getting child support. Child support, substance or finances, earned by her husband that should have been used for their household, given to her and her kids. This is now, after this woman has been on many of these yearly trips. And now it is time for another trip. Yes, it's that time of year again, and she could already feel herself getting sick.

This yearly trip is one of the three that Deuteronomy 16:1-17 shares with us that Israelite men were required to travel once a year to the Temple at Shiloh, which Joshua established for the Lord in Joshua 18. We learned there that it was at the Temple that the men were to partake in each of these feasts. If they were able financially to do so, they were required to bring their wives and their children, and it is now time for yet another feast.

This particular feast was most likely the Feast of the Tabernacles, and Elkanah, being the godly man that he was and the apparent man of means who could afford to travel with two wives, brings both of his wives and his children, that is, Hannah and Peninnah and her children. When they arrive the Bible informs us that it was Elkanah's custom to give portions of the sacrifice to Peninnah and each of her kids. After all, he, as the head of the house, made sacrifice to God for them, and he provided her with enough food to feed her and the kids. After he'd done this the Bible reports that he would also give portion to Hannah; however, the Bible makes a distinct difference. It says that to Hannah he would give double portion. The reason that it says that he gave Hannah twice as much as he gave Peninnah was simply "because he loved her" (1 Samuel 1:5).

Hannah got double roses on Valentine's Day; she got a full dozen, while the other woman simply got six. She was the one who got double the quality time, double the substance, double the portion, double the exposure, double the compliments, double the accolades, double the conversation, and double the intimacy. The Bible says he gave her double because he loved her. Even though she could not have kids, he loved her enough to give her double.

But watch this! Even though the other wife, Peninnah, only got half of the portion that Hannah got, half of the relationship that Hannah received, half of the face time that she got; even though she got a few hours during the week while Hannah got extended weekends; even though she got half of the financial support, compliments, and conversation, the Bible declares that she had the nerve to torment Hannah because the Lord had closed Hannah's womb. Peninnah knew that if Hannah could have had kids then Peninnah wouldn't even be here, because it was clear whom the father of her children loved. So Peninnah would torment Hannah because she could not have kids. In fact, the text says that every year during the trip Peninnah would torment Hannah, and here it is that time of the year again, and I believe Hannah could already feel herself getting sick. Hannah is experiencing Baby Mama Drama.

Now the Bible doesn't say it, but I was just thinking, how did she torment her? If we exegete this text through the hermeneutical lens of 21st-century relationships we can come up with a few suggestions on how she would torment her. Furthermore, with that lens we might even locate the origin of some of the torment that many of us deal with today. Could it be that Peninnah was calling Elkanah to come by and see the kids on days that she knew he was supposed to be with Hannah? Or maybe she would call their house late at night in order to talk? Maybe she would tell Elkanah Jr. and Little Penny that Hannah was the reason that they could not see their daddy as often as they wanted. Maybe she told them that if only they would break up they could have their daddy at home.

So the kids begin to treat their stepmother with hostility. Again the Bible doesn't say it, but I was just thinking. Maybe Peninnah is always complaining about the money that he has been giving her every month or spending it on herself and not on the kids. Of course, while she is doing this, she maybe reminds her children that he's doing more for Hannah than he is doing for us. Could this be why she is busting out the car windows of his new wife? Is this why she is constantly going to juvenile court to ask for more money? The Bible doesn't say how she tormented her but what it does say is that every year Peninnah would torment Hannah. This was Baby Mama Drama.

Furthermore, we know that this exchange was so serious that Hannah would burst out into tears and refuse to eat. Before I go further I need to hang out here homiletically for a minute because this story that I am sharing is eerily familiar to some of the stories that we live today. Hannah is crying and refusing to eat because her husband's Baby Mama is tormenting her. Though she knows her husband loves her, though she has the nice house and car, though he has given her double portion, she is dealing with Baby Mama Drama. Elkanah notices that she is tormented and comes to address it in the 8th verse of the chapter and says, "What are you crying about? It is no secret that I love you more than anything. Why are you not eating? Why is your heart so sad? Isn't being married to me better than ten sons? Isn't what you have better than what you want?"

What made the Drama so bad? Well, the Bible doesn't say, but I was just thinking. I believe that Baby Mama Drama is on both sides. In a real sense, Baby Mama Drama deals with a grass-is-greener principle; it deals with women who are fighting to be in, or fighting, the position of another woman. Hannah was dealing with Drama, but so was Peninnah. You see, though Hannah was receiving double the substance, and even though Elkanah clearly loved her more, Peninnah had given him something that she could not give him. But on the other side, though Peninnah had given him the children that Hannah could not, Peninnah was tormenting Hannah because she was receiving more substance or symbols of love. I mean, Peninnah had the babies but someone else get the house and picket fence. She went through labor, but she doesn't get the Christmas tree and stockings.

But Hannah, she had the house but not the seed. She had the love and stuff but could never have the firstborn. Elkanah Jr. was not her son and is a constant reminder of her man's seed through someone else. All of this, however, pales in comparison in my estimation to the real problem. The real problem is that, year after year, Peninnah would torment Hannah, and the Bible doesn't record one time that Elkanah would handle his business. He was the one who should have dealt with Peninnah. Can't you hear Hannah asking him, "Why are you putting up with this? I mean, I know what that Heifer is up to. Why do you keep defending her and taking up for her against me? You know that she is dogging me out and you have not said anything!"

Hannah could not take it any longer. She refused to continue to allow her happiness to be in the hands of someone else. She realized that she had given her power away. She realized that she had been taking her problems to the wrong place, and she decided to take her stuff now to the Lord. It is at that moment that her motives changed. She decided that she no longer wanted to get even; she did not want to have a child so that her child would outdo Peninnah's. But she prayed to the Lord, "God, since my name means grace, I need some grace. God, I am not hating on nobody; it isn't about anybody else, but Lord, it's me standing in the need of prayer. God, while on others Thou art calling, please don't pass me by."

She went into the Temple after the feast. No one was there except the priest. She poured out her soul to the Lord. Oh, if we could have listened to what her soul said to the Lord. Maybe she said,

"Lord, I hear of showers of blessings Thou art scattering full and free, showers upon the thirsty souls refreshing. Let some drops now fall on me." She poured out her soul to the Lord, "God, give me a child and I will give him back to you." While she was praying the priest Eli was observing her. And he noticed that while her mouth was moving nothing was coming out. He assumed that she was drunk. He confronted and accused her of being drunk. She said, "Why do you think I am drunk?" He said, "Because when you were praying I could not hear what you were saying." I just believe in my sanctified imagination that she said, "I don't mean any disrespect, but the reason that you didn't hear me is because I wasn't talking to you."

She knew that she had relied on others long enough. Most likely she had tried to talk to Peninnah and she had tried to talk to Elkanah. She even tried to talk to the doctors and then she decided this must be a job for the Lord. I bet it was then that a few hymns came to mind . . . songs like "Have a little talk with Jesus, tell him all about your struggles. He'll hear your faintest cry and answer by and by. Feel a little prayer wheel turning and know that the fire is burning. Just have a little talk with Jesus and it makes it right."

Maybe it wasn't that one, maybe it was: "I must tell Jesus all of my troubles. I cannot bear these burdens alone. In my distress he kindly will help me. He ever loves and cares for his own." And is there anybody here who can attest to the fact that when you take your burdens to the Lord, He will? Oh Yes, He will!

8

Sleeping with the Enemy

There was a wealthy man from Maon who owned property near the town of Carmel. He had 3,000 sheep and 1,000 goats, and it was sheep-shearing time. This man's name was Nabal, and his wife, Abigail, was a sensible and beautiful woman. But Nabal, a descendant of Caleb, was crude and mean in all his dealings (1 Samuel 25:2-3, NLT).

"It's a girl!" This is the beautiful announcement at the birth of a daughter. This heralding statement means that prayers have been answered, and the revelation is that the nursery needs to be pink and not blue. For the man, there is a fantastic feeling of fear and joy that he is a father, while there are mixed emotions of completion and commencement for a mother. Her body is finally hers again and in one sense it is over, but at the same time her heart will never be hers again and this is only the beginning. All because of the announcement of "It's a girl!"

It is at this moment that responsible parents begin to plot out what the child's life should be like. In a real sense they begin to wish, hope, and pray for the best. Whenever they look at the child, provision and protection is their first thought. How can I work more overtime or move to a better, safer neighborhood? The plans that they have for the child are great. The child will excel in their advancement, hopefully doing way better than the parents. She, of course, will be smarter than the average kid, breezing through the work. She will get good grades, do well in sports, and be liked and popular. She will go to and graduate from college, of course pledging the same sorority as her mother, and eventually meeting and falling in love with someone who will fall in love with her. This is a perfect scenario, and all of this is implied and/or dreamed about with the announcement of "It's a girl!"

Never in a million years would the parents expect that their daughter would be the author of this letter:

To the Members at the Place of the Outpouring,

In the beginning, I was young . . . he was handsome. He said I was beautiful, that I was smart, worthy of love . . . That is how I was made to feel and so we were married, walking joyfully together down a church aisle, our union was seemingly blessed by God.

Then came the angry words . . . the verbal tearing apart . . . Now I was made to feel ugly, unintelligent, unworthy of any love, God's or man's. He said that I was too fat after the kids came. None of my meals were good enough. He told me I was stupid even though I have a Master's Degree. I mean, how could he call me lazy when I was the one who worked while he went to school? How could he be so mean?

Next came the beatings . . . unrelenting violence . . .
   unceasing pain.
I said that I shouldn't stay, but this is my husband . . .
   promised forever.
He said I deserve it. Maybe I do. If I could just be
   good . . . I feel alone.

Where is God? Doesn't He hear me when I cry out
silently as I lie in bed each night?
I think I just need to pray about this thing.
There is so much I want to . . . SSSSHHH . . . . he's
coming. I will write later.
—Abigail

Though this letter possibly could have been written by any
female or any male, the signature of Abigail transports us back-
wards through the tunnels of time and the hallways of history to
the beautiful and plush fields of the Central Palestinian hillside village of Carmel and to the residence of the successful entrepreneur
and agribusiness man named Nabal.

Now the Bible tells us three distinct things about Nabal: one is
that he was a wealthy man; two, that he was married to a fine and
intelligent sister named Abigail; and three, that he was harsh, he
was mean, and he was even evil in his dealings. He was a mean rich
brother who was married to a fine, smart sister named Abigail,
whose name means "my father's joy." It is the mind of Abigail that
I believe wrote this letter to us today. As we begin to look at this
letter, notice the tone of the voice in each paragraph. It is almost as
if this woman is two different women.

I mean, in the beginning there was a happy woman, excited to
be with her man. He encouraged her and said that she was beautiful, and she believed him. She was intelligent. Maybe they met in
grad school. However, when they fell in love, he convinced her that
she would not have to work, so she traded in her dreams and aspirations in order to support his dreams of being a business owner.
She was fine. He had a trophy wife. Then she conceived and bore
him children and raised them while he was working. After many
days of hard work, he becomes what many consider an instant success. Everything should be great, and that is when the voice of the
second woman shows up.

For some reason, things change drastically and dramatically. She tells us that the compliments have turned into complaints; the food that used to be delicious has become distasteful. Now he is putting her down and calling her out of her name. She felt her self-esteem start to suffer. After all, she relied on him for so much, now she feels herself falling into depression. She used to have friends, but in order to please him she gave them all up. Now she is by herself constantly and is consistently being verbally beaten up and beaten down. She goes to church and gets a weekly up lift, but he tears up the church and church people. When she garners enough strength to speak up for herself and in defense of the pastor, church, and people who have kept her in the game that is when it escalates and WHAM!!! He hits her and beats her. She's tired of hurting, and in her pain she wants to leave, but she scared as hell and doesn't know what he will do.

Or she decides to endure it until the kids get grown. After all, she can't pay all of the bills by herself. When she shares it with pseudo-religious pastors they don't offer any informed commentary; they simply give her an old answer to a new question by saying, "Just pray" or "The Lord will make a way." She can't tell anybody in the family because she is embarrassed. Somehow she believes that her husband might be right. Maybe it is her fault and somehow she brought it on herself. If only she had not been so late coming home—9:30 is late. What if she was quieter? If only she had read the recipe better, worked out harder, or not bothered him so much. If only she wore a longer skirt then the other men would not have looked at her. And where is God? Can't you hear the voices of this woman? Of Abigail?

Beloved, I must admit that I cannot truthfully say with assurance that all of this happened in Abigail's life. In fact, the biblical story is that King David and 400 of his men were returning from the Prophet Samuel's funeral in Ramah. This was deep for David because in many ways Samuel was his father in the ministry. He and his men served as mercenaries and had been watching the sheep and the servants of the rich people in Carmel, protecting them from the Philistines. When David and his men ran out of supplies, they would appeal to those whom they protected for support. The record is that when they went to Nabal, David's servants greeted him with respect and wished him long life. But Nabal, in his arrogance, plays them off. He said, "Who is your David? Who is this Son of Jesse?" David is mad and gets his men ready to wage war against Nabal, vowing to kill all of the men. While he is getting ready to go and fight, a servant tells Abigail that her husband messed up. The Bible says that she gathers an offering together and takes it to King David. In verse 23, she falls on her knees and says not to pay attention to this worthless man Nabal. She even said his name is Nabal and he personifies his name. It must be noted that the name Nabal meant fool.

So literally she says to David, don't waste your time with this mean fool. She pleads for the King not to destroy the house and he does not. This is basically all the text says, that the man was a rich, mean, foolish man who was married to a fine sister. He was arrogant enough to diss the King. So I don't know if all of the abuse that I talked about actually happened to Abigail. However, as I consider the traits and actions of the Nabal in the text and the fact that 25–35% of Christian couples have dealt with, are dealing with, or will deal with abuse, and the fact that 3.5 million women are beaten in their homes every year and more than 2,000 a year are murdered by their partners—I know that if it did not happen to Abigail, it has or is happening to someone in here.

What is amazing is that you don't know what went wrong. Like the first voice of Abigail, everything was fine in the marriage or maybe you are not married. Maybe you are in high school and you call yourself liking someone, and your parents meet him and they say it's cool. Everything seems cool when you go to the game together. But all of a sudden you start noticing some of the traits of an abuser. I mean, he becomes super jealous and wants to know where you are all of the time. He calls and texts your phone over and over again and goes off when you don't respond. He wants to monopolize your time and forces you into isolation by not wanting you to be with anybody else—family or friends. He always gets mad and emotionally charged up when he doesn't get his way. Since he cannot take criticism, he begins to criticize you. Because of some unresolved inefficiency in himself and because he doesn't have it all together, he tries to tear you apart. That's when he crosses the psychological barrier and become a potential physical abuser. It is when he says something along these lines: "If you leave me I will kill myself" or "I love you so much that if I can't have you nobody will, because nobody will ever love you like I love you."

It is this rhetoric of verbal abuse that begins to serve as crossover into physical abuse. For when they begin to speak of hurting you, it creates images of hurting you. If they can see it they will definitely do it—it is just a matter of time. That is when the grabbing, the slapping, the hitting, punching, and kicking starts. This is followed by the muffing and the choking, and most of the time this type of activity ends in the hospital or the cemetery. 3.5 million females are beaten and over 2,000 women are murdered by the hands of the ones they love, and what trips me out is that, like Abigail, the woman knows that the man she is with is a fool.

The man that she fell in love with was one who used to live life by the standards of the Word of God. He seemingly used to believe Colossians 3:19: "And you husbands must love your wives and never treat them harshly." He used to believe that his blessings were somehow tied to how he treated his wife, like it says in 1 Peter 3:7: "In the same way, you husbands must give honor to your wives. Treat her with understanding as you live together. She may be weaker than you are, but she is your equal partner in God's gift of new life. If you don't treat her as you should, your prayers will not be heard." But now he has lost all of the knowledge of God, and like Abigail says, he is simply rendered a fool.

But I believe that though it might take a while, there comes a time for some when the abused look at the abuser and say, "Enough is enough! I've taken all I am gon' take and I have done it for the last time. I tried and tried but now I'm sick and I am tired. I can't take it anymore. You've hit me for the last time. You ain't puttin' your hands on me no more. I refuse to continue to play myself down so you can feel good. No! No! I am just as smart or smarter than you. And another thing, you can't cuss me out anymore. I have been called the last whore, bitch, and slut that I'm gon' be called. That ain't what my parents named me and that ain't what I'm gon' answer to. I can't take it anymore."

This is what I would argue that Abigail thought when she heard how Nabal treated the King. Now the Bible doesn't say this, but I was just thinking that she picked up her pen and begin to write the final piece to her letter. She says:

> Hey y'all, it's me again, and I wanted to give you an update on my situation. I know that I sounded bad and down last time, but let me tell you what happened. In one of my lowest moments of feeling beaten, hurt, and worthless, I just wanted to end it and kill myself. But then I saw one of my baby pictures. I looked into a mirror and I remembered that I was the same beautiful person in the picture. It's been a lot of years and I have my own kids now, but I realized that I was still my mother's pride and my father's joy. Finally came the release, the realization. It's not me . . . it's him. . . . I am beautifully and wonderfully made. I am worthy of love, both God's and man's. I cannot look for someone else to give to me what I should have myself. I am my

own cheering squad. I am what I believe me to be. God loved me enough to save me when I wanted to die, and I love God enough to live life to the fullest of my possibility.
Thanks for listening,
Abigail

This is what shouts to me about the text and about Abigail and even about those in here who has dealt with abuse or deal with it all the time. The shout is that even while hurting, even while depressed, even while knowingly married to a fool, she still had enough sense to take a gift to the King. She still had enough sense to come and lay her requests at the King's feet. Even though she did not know how everything would work out, she still had the mind enough to bring her best and lay it at the King's feet.

I wish I had one or two people who knew what I was talking about. That when things in your life were seemingly at their worst and life had beaten you up and beaten you down, you were able to get into the presence of the King and offer gifts. When I come into this house, I lift up both my hands, humble myself, and I begin to worship Him . . .

9
Living Beyond My Violation

by Dr. Rosalyn Nichols
Senior Pastor of Freedom's Chapel Christian Church,
Memphis, Tennessee

(Now she was wearing a long robe with sleeves; for this is how the virgin daughters of the king were clothed in earlier times.) So his servant put her out, and bolted the door after her. But Tamar put ashes on her head, and tore the long robe that she was wearing; she put her hand on her head, and went away, crying aloud as she went. Her brother Absalom said to her, "Has Amnon your brother been with you? Be quiet for now, my sister; he is your brother; do not take this to heart." So Tamar remained, a desolate woman, in her brother Absalom's house. When King David heard of all these things, he became very angry, but he would not punish his son Amnon, because he loved him, for he was his firstborn. But Absalom spoke to Amnon neither good nor bad; for Absalom hated Amnon, because he had raped his sister Tamar (2 Samuel 13:18-22, NRSV).

There were born to Absalom three sons, and one daughter whose name was Tamar; she was a beautiful woman (2 Samuel 14:27, NRSV).

He grabbed me! I reached out to hand him the cakes he asked me to cook for him. They said he was sick. He was sick, so I went. I cooked. I gave him what he asked for, but he grabbed me. I reached to hand him the cakes and he took hold of me. It did not seem real. I thought I was dreaming. What was happening to me?

I felt the plate I held out to him slip from my hands. The edge of one of the cakes touched my fingers as it slid from the plate and fell to the floor. He pulled me down towards him to the bed. He caught me so off-guard, I fell forward, and as I did I felt the hot, moist heat from his breath against my neck as he whispered in my ear, "Come, lie with me, my sister." I cried out "No!" I struggled to pull away, but he was strong. He would not let me go. There was no one there to hear me, no one there to see him. He had sent them all away. We were alone. The doors were closed. No one heard me; no one saw.

I tried to reason with him. I tried to stay calm. "No, my brother, do not force me; for such a thing is not done in Israel; do not do anything so vile!" After all, we were the King's children. This was not supposed to happen in the king's household. I was the king's daughter. He was the king's son. This was not how we were raised. This was not the kind of thing we are supposed to do. But he wouldn't listen. The more I pleaded, the tighter his grip. He held me against himself and I could feel my heart beating against his chest. The musk of his body filled my nostrils and made me sick. But I kept talking. I kept trying to make him let me go. I wanted him to think about the consequences. I wanted to make him stop.

What about me? Where could I carry my shame? My mind was racing. I am a virgin in my father's house. I have not married or bore children. I will have no honor. I will be humiliated. No man will want me. Like a broken cistern that holds no water, I will be broken. How can I live beyond my pain?

That's when I realized he didn't care about me. I saw it in his eyes. They were filled with sick desire, like a ravenous animal in search of prey. It was as if his teeth had become fangs. His hands against my skin felt like paws. He didn't care about me, but what about him? I said to him, "And as for you, you would be as one of the fools, a scoundrel in Israel."

Hearing these words he held me tighter, and I could feel him growing stronger. Like a cobra ready to strike, he was rigid and unyielding. Maybe if he sees another way. Maybe I can convince him it's ok, just not this way. I took a deep breath and looked into his eyes and said, "Now therefore, I beg you, speak to the king; for he will not withhold me from you." But he would not listen. The more I begged and pleaded, he would not listen. The more I tried to persuade him, he would not listen, and he was stronger than me. I hated it. I hated that he was stronger than me. That he had grabbed me. That he took hold of me. I hated that he put me in this position. This was not a stranger. This was not a neighbor. This was family! This was not on the road, at the market, in some dark corner. This was in his home.

I lay there and hated him for what he took from me. I hated him for violating me. I hated that my innocence was snatched; my trust was crushed; my kindness became my weakness; my upbringing was my undoing. I hated that he would not listen, and that he was stronger than me. He forced me down on his bed and he raped me. He laid me there and raped me. I said NO! But he raped me just the same.

And when he was done it was as if the fever broke. However, instead of coming to his senses, instead of the weight of shame resting on him, instead of his sinfulness consuming him, he hated me. I watched it wash over him. It was as if the hate went out of me and spread to him. He looked at me with eyes of loathing and contempt. I saw the spirit come over him. I watched it grow. It filled the room and I was more terrified than even before. "Get out!" he said to me. The beautiful evidence of my virginity was tarnished by and mixed with his uncleanness. The moist mixture coated my skin like some kind of evil and despicable badge of shame.

"No, my brother," I said, as tears streamed down my face, "for this wrong in sending me away is greater than the other that you did to me!" He wanted to me to leave like a whore—not like family, but like some scandalous woman he had innocently brought in from the street. He wanted to put me out as if I had done him wrong. "NO!" I said. But he would not listen. He called the young man who served him and said, "Put this woman out of my presence, and bolt the door after her."

Tamar was raped; young, beautiful, and naive Tamar. Tamar was victimized by a family and a society that has a psychological expectation that women are at the disposal of men, that women can be preyed upon by men, and that women are nothing more than a means to an end for men. Tamar was raped, y'all!

According to the Center for Disease Control, 1 in 4 girls is sexually abused before the age of 18. In 8 out of 10 rape cases, the victim knows the perpetrator. A 2002 Tufts University study reported that the number one killer of African American women ages 15 to 34 is homicide at the hands of a current or former intimate partner. Tamar was raped by a society that despite her given name did not consider her precious enough to protect.

And how does Tamar respond? What does Tamar do after the world violated her? How does Tamar react? As the servant rushed her broken body out the door, the long dress that she confidently wore to tell the world that she was the pure, unconquered daughter of the king is now bloodied and soiled by the heinous act. How does Tamar react? The click of the door is a deafening sound that everything now has forever changed. The word says, "Tamar put ashes on her head, and tore the long robe that she was wearing; she put her hand on her head, and went away, crying aloud as she went."

I suggest that there are many Tamars in our society. They are women who have had the fabric of their innocence torn away; it has been stolen or they have traded it, only replaced it with the ashes of pain, crying, and wailing as they make their way. We see Tamar every day. Violated women, beautiful, well-dressed, coifed, groomed, well educated, but violated . . . with the ashes of pain still on them. Reaching with their hands to cover and hide the shame; with the tears of sorrow and grief covered only by their makeup, with their bags filled with tissue and regret.

And how do we respond to Tamar? What does her family say? What do we say when Tamar gets raped in our homes, in our communities, in our schools, in our pews? Some of us are Amnon—we turn our lust into hate, bolt the door on Tamar, and refuse to see her, hear her, or even listen to her. Others of us are the king. We react to Tamar and the news of the tragedy in the way that King David did. The Bible says that when King David heard of all these things, he became very angry, but he would not punish his son Amnon, because he loved him, for he was his firstborn. There are too many Davids who choose love over justice, and in so doing sacrifice Tamar without even a glimpse of mercy.

Some of us are Absalom. Even in love we want Tamar to keep silent; Absalom said, "Be quiet for now, my sister; he is your brother; do not take this to heart." How many Absaloms have asked Tamar to be quiet and not take it to heart? How many Absaloms, out of love and ignorance, have asked Tamar not to speak, not to do the very thing that victims need to do to find justice for themselves? How many Absaloms have unintentionally made silence a fresh wound when the voice of the victim so desperately needs to be heard?

Actress and comedian Mo'Nique confessed to the world a few years ago that her older brother had molested her. She said, "I confronted him and told my parents, he said I was lying, and nothing was really done." No one in her family, neither her father nor her mother, chose to hear the pain in Mo'Nique's story. No one who said they loved her was willing to listen to her! Year after year, no matter how successful she appeared on the outside, she carried her story on the inside. She could mask the scars on the outside, but it would only be in the sharing of her story that she could healing begin on the inside!

The word of God says, "So Tamar remained, a desolate woman, in her brother Absalom's house." How many women in the path of Tamar have been left as desolate women because of the pain they have not been allowed to express? How many are still in pain, at the family gatherings in pain, at the family functions in pain, in the family circle in pain? How many Tamars have we labeled and left desolate women because we don't want to have to deal with their pain? What is the fall out for the Tamars of the world?

How does Tamar deal with the pain in her heart and the labels we give her? How does Tamar respond? How does Tamar react? When you see Tamar in the village, what does she say to you? Listen and you'll hear her say, in the words of Maya Angelou:

> You may write me down in history
> With your bitter, twisted lies,
> You may trod me in the very dirt
> But still, like dust, I'll rise.[1]

Listen and you'll hear Tamar say, in the words of Alice Walker:

> Be nobody's darling;
> Be an outcast.
> Take the contradictions
> Of your life
> And wrap around
> You like a shawl[2]

Listen to Tamar as she says, in the words of Oprah: "The struggle of my life created empathy—I could relate to pain, being abandoned, having people not love me."[3]

From Maya Angelou to Alice Walker, from Mo'Nique to Oprah, the voice of Tamar refuses to be silent, refuses to accept the labels placed upon her! She takes her wounds and turns them into wisdom, wisdom not for herself, but for the Tamars who will come after her.

And that wisdom did not stay in Absalom's home. Oh, I believe that the story didn't end with this woman as a desolate woman!

I believe that the legacy of the kind of women who don't let men have the last say lived beyond the walls of Absalom's home. While the men battled it out, Tamar worked it out. The word says, "There were born to Absalom three sons, and one daughter whose name was Tamar; she was a beautiful woman." I believe that baby girl grew up with an aunt who taught her not how to submit but how to resist. Not how to be quiet, but to speak up. Not to live in the shadow of brutality, but to live in the beauty of one who would come and give new life more abundantly.

I believe, even in the house, Tamar believed and taught her little niece the words of her faith, the words of the prophet: "Comfort, O comfort my people, says your God. Speak tenderly to Jerusalem, and cry to her that she has served her term" (Isaiah 40:1-2, NRSV).

I believe that Tamar kept the words her father spoke hidden in her heart, and she said, "Vindicate me, O Lord, for I have walked in my integrity, and I have trusted in the Lord without wavering. Prove me, O Lord, and try me; test my heart and mind. For your steadfast love is before my eyes, and I walk in faithfulness to you" (Psalm 26:1-3, NRSV).

I believe that Tamar poured herself into the little girl who watched and learned how to live beyond desolation to consecration, beyond wounds to wisdom, beyond brutality back to beauty.

And the legacy of Tamar lives on, I tell you! When a young girl on a school bus in Rutherford County in Nashville cries out "NO!," Tamar lives beyond her violation!

When we stand in solidarity with the women who were raped and mutilated in silence and humiliation in the Congo, in Afghanistan, and the Sudan, Tamar lives beyond her violation.

Each time a woman refuses to allow the lustful choices of a man to ruin her life, Tamar lives beyond her violation.

Each time, rather than be quiet, a woman is encouraged to wear her ashes, utter her grief, express her pain, and speak out loud about her trauma, then Tamar lives beyond her violation.

Today we are here because we are determined that Tamar's story will not end in desolation. We are confident that Tamar's story will not end in despondency.

We are here for all the Tamars of this world, for those women who have been raped in this life; who have been violated in this life; who have had their innocence snatched from them; who have been played by the subjugating systems of this world. We are here for all the Tamars of this world, for the babies raped by men convinced that their virginity will cure them of HIV/AIDS; for the girls gang raped on the school bus; for the little girls seduced, tricked, lied to, and lied on the playground; for the women on Craigslist, FB, and Twitter being texted and harassed, stalked and assaulted.

I'm here for Tamar! I'm here to tell Tamar what Absalom didn't know how to tell her, what Amnon wasn't man enough to give her, what David was too arrogant to provide her. I'm here to give Tamar what Jesus gave me. I'm here to offer what he gave that woman at the well that was blessed by a man who knew all her stuff and loved her because her stuff didn't matter. I'm here to give her what Jesus gave me.

I'm here to tell that Tamar you did not sin! I'm here to tell Tamar, You are blessed among women! I'm here to tell Tamar, Your name is written in the Lamb's book of Life! I'm here to tell Tamar, Your robe has been washed clean in the blood of the Lamb and God will wipe every tear from your eye!

I'm here to tell her, I know a man who knows all about you and loves you! I'm here to give you what a man named Jesus gave me: power, love, and a sound mind! Peace that passes all understanding! Joy that the world can't give and the world can't take away! I'm here because the potter wants to put you back together again!!! Come out, Tamar . . . come out! Come on out of the house, Tamar! Walk in the light, beautiful light. Come where the dewdrops of mercy shine bright, shine all around us by day and by night . . . Jesus, the light of the world!

Notes

1. Maya Angelou, "Still I Rise."
http://www.poemhunter.com/poem/still-i-rise/.

2. Alice Walker, "Be Nobody's Darling."
http://www.poemhunter.com/poem/be-nobody-s-darling/.

3. http://www.brainyquote.com/quotes/quotes/o/oprahwinfr417338.html.

10

Waiting to Exhale:
Savannah and the Curse of Eve

To the woman he said, "I will greatly increase your pangs in childbearing; in pain you shall bring forth children, yet your desire shall be for your husband, And he shall rule over you" (Genesis 3:16, NRSV).

It's New Year's Eve and the city is bustling. Everyone's excited about the fact that once again they have the opportunity to watch the old go out and the new come in. People are planning which parties they will attend and/or which church services they will go to. Others have decided not to mess with the rush of people. Instead, they will simply stay in and have a wonderful dinner for many or an intimate meal for two over some champagne while watching the iconic *Dick Clark's Rockin' New Year's Eve*, as he counts down into the New Year in Times Square, New York. Excitement is in the air because it was New Year's Eve and across the country every city was bustling, and the case was no different in the metro area of Phoenix, Arizona, where everybody who is anybody was listening to the smooth sounds of K107.

I mean, this was the station and sound that informed those in the know of where the best of the best hung out and partied. In a real sense, you cannot be a card-carrying member of the Black Elite, either by look or by income, bringing in the New Year with just anybody, so they listened to K107 to make sure they were directed to the right place. It was through subtle nuances that range from the artists played to the mention of a hefty cover charge that the DJ conveyed the message that directed the ghetto people to the ghetto parties as well as the bougsies to where they need to be.

Such was the case for a 32-year-old beautiful new Denver transplant to the Phoenix community, a television producer by the name of Savannah. Armed with a New Year's resolution, Savannah arrives at an exclusive type of buppie New Year's Eve party to meet a blind date by the name of Lionel. She has no idea that he showed up to meet her with another woman.

Ladies and Gentleman, welcome to the first in the *Waiting to Exhale* Series, in which we attempt to exegete an intersection of the Bible and the reality of the normalcy of dysfunction in human relationships and interactions as portrayed in the Forrest Whitaker 1995 cinematic release, *Waiting to Exhale*. The movie, as I am sure you remember, chronicled the relationship of four African American women at different stages in life. They were at different levels of financial independence and different places of emotion, maturity, and security. Bernadine, Gloria, Robin, and Savannah had individual identities and idiosyncrasies. They had ups and downs that, in their search for happiness, success, and companionship, resonated so loud in the lives of women as well as men that *Waiting to Exhale* was a more-than-anticipated smash hit.

However, if you noticed, my chosen order of naming the characters was, I'm sure, different than what you expected. For rhetorical purposes I named them in alphabetical order as not to cast more importance on one character or typology than on another. However, if there is anyone in the building this morning who saw the movie I'm sure that, based on the lens of their own history and experience, they would argue that alphabetical order was in no way the order of importance.

I mean, I believe that some would say that Gloria, the single mother who ends up with Gregory Hines after facing and admitting the painful reality of her co-dependent relationship with her son, is most important. Others would argue that Bernadine, the unexpected divorcee whose husband endeavored to leave her with nothing after two kids and 11 years of marriage, is the character of most import. While still others of us, especially our youth and young adults, would posit and agree that it's the ultra-hot, many-times-Spandex-clad Robin who speaks most profoundly to their reality. However, though I don't discount any of those views, I believe that if one endeavors to homiletically treat this movie and the characters therein, it behooves them to deal with whom I have deemed the most complex of the four characters and really the focal point of the movie: Savannah.

Played by Whitney Houston, Savannah, I believe, is the darling to most viewers. Just moving from Denver to the Phoenix area, Savannah has almost everything she wants, in that she not only has a history in television but now she has her dream job as a producer. For her, things seemingly cannot be any better; however, there is something missing for Ms. Savannah. Even though her beauty seemingly makes her the want of every man and the envy of every woman; even though she has more than a respectable income, which clearly affords all of what she needs and most of what she wants; and even though it appears that her life is complete, the truth of the matter is that there is something that she longs for that she does not have. In fact, the reality of her desire for this particular thing in her life is so strong that her need became the main motive for her move from Denver to Phoenix. If you don't believe me, you only need to listen to her testimony that were the first words of dialogue that take place after the credits have rolled. She said, and I'm paraphrasing, the men in Denver are dead, and I will try Phoenix men.

When she arrives, she has a new job, in a new town, and a desire for a man. She is a fine 30-something-year-old sister in a new town, making money, dressed nice and rubbing elbows with the right people, flowing in the right crowd. This is what the movie shows us. But what we don't see is Savannah's inner desire for something else, something that fills a void, a void that in Savannah's history and mindset convinces her that she needs a man. Now before the new school and pseudo-liberated women hearing or reading this get an attitude and think that this sermon is going in a direction that is to you unacceptable, or before you think that I am trying to paint all of you sisters in what you think is the same chasm of a sweeping and demoralizing generalization, please allow me to once again use the words of Savannah herself as she begins to describe her own situation.

She says she has been looking for a good man for some time now, and the problem is that she cannot find anyone with compassion, purpose, and integrity. She said that in her search she has ended up with more than just one disappointment; she has had Robert, Cedric, and Darryl, and all have been strikeouts. The problem, she believes, is that men only act like they know what a woman needs. All the while, she believes, it is the goal of most men to make the woman feel and believe that she is desperate. "HELL NO! NOT ME" she says to herself as she walks into the hotel party on New Year's Eve to meet Lionel, a man that only her ears know; one whose voice was intriguing enough to meet and be with, at least for tonight.

She's there early and sees an open seat and asks if the seat is open. Her question is, of course, met by the eyes and smiles of welcoming men who are willing for her to have the seat. However, their dates were way less than OK with that. In fact, their scouring looks told the whole story, and being the woman she was, Savannah let us know in her narrative monologue how she felt about these haterettes and what they said through their looks. She said, "That's right, ladies, I'm here, and if you don't like it, too bad. I'm here and I am fine, and if you are not careful and if you turn your head one time I will have your man. Because [and these are her words] I am single and desperate and have no morals."

As the tension builds at the table, Savannah gets up and meets her reason for being there, Lionel. Upon meeting Lionel, Savannah thanks God because his appearance is all that she wanted, and after some conversation he asks her to dance. And it was as he pulls her close and she feels him for the first time that she exhales. An exhale . . . the breath she has been holding for that special one. An exhale . . . the tension of life that one only releases when they know that they have something sure—that cigarette after a meal or that breath after that first sip of beer after a hard day's work.

She exhaled!!!! After Robert, Cedric, Darryl, and others, she thought this was the one, and she exhaled. This would be cool if she really thought he was the one, but it was her words that messed me up and added the complexity to the movie, to the character, and even to this sermon. She says that as she held him she pretended that she was with someone else and it was good.

OK, I have a question . . . Are you serious? Do women really do that, wait to exhale? Do women hold their breath waiting and wanting a man or a partner who will be worthy of the sigh of relief and release? But then if the object of their desire is not available, will they really fake breathing with someone else and in essence cheat themselves and rob whomever they're with of a meaningful experience?

By the way, Savannah, who is this dude you exhaled for? I mean, we saw how even though Lionel dissed you by showing up to your date with another woman, you still invited him over for a special evening. Though he disrespected your home by using your toothbrush, you were OK and seemingly took that all in stride. In fact, the only thing you said to us was, "Hell, it's been five months and he's gotten on my last nerves, but I don't have to be in love with him to do it to him. Hell, my body needs this." Then we saw that after that sexual encounter you let Lionel go.

Who is it, Savannah? Who is this dude worthy of an exhale, worthy of that which you have been holding for that special moment? Who is the one who is worthy of your essence, your specialness? There is a sister here asking, like Savannah, who is worthy of my intimacy, my mind, my body, my soul, my house, my children, my life, my credit, my virginity, my dreams, my fears? Who is worthy of my exhale?

There are some sisters in here right now wanting to shout or to cry because you are looking back over your life thinking of those you deemed worthy; whether they were the real one or the one you pretended that he was. Ironically, at the same time, there are some brothers in here right now who are likewise wondering if the exhale you have gotten was indeed your exhale or secretly was your boo exhaling for someone else.

Savannah, who is he? You know that the movie does not make us wait long before Kenneth, a married blast from Savannah's past, shows up with the help of her mother, who gave Kenneth Savannah's number because he will be soon be traveling to Phoenix. When Savannah tells her mother that she was wrong for sharing her number with a happily married man, her mother's response begins to shape the sermonic lens. Her mother said, "Well, he must not be that happy . . . Plus I don't want you to end up like me—old, single, and without a man." Though she protested the call due to some morals and past pain, Savannah, she who has everything and really needs no drama, invites and entertains drama. Why would she do that? Why would she allow her desire to rule over her? I mean, even though her mother, based upon her own needs, thinks it's OK, does that make it OK? She knows what is right. Why is her desire so strong?

And God came walking through the garden in what the Bible says was the cool of the evening looking for his longtime friend

Adam and his new unnamed wife. God is looking for them because they were not in their usual places for their evening walk. You see, God enjoyed such a relationship with His creation that every evening God and man would be together. God and Adam enjoyed unchecked relationship until God realized that it was not good for man to be alone. He caused a sleep to come upon the man and took a rib from him and formed (built) woman from the rib and presented her to man. From that time they were one and they enjoyed God's friendship in the Garden. All of it was theirs like it was God's; they did not have to plant trees, but they ate the fruits. They did not have to build houses, but they were covered by heavens and the trees formed for them a canopy. However, there was one tree that they were not supposed to eat from, but they did. Here it is that in the cool of the evening that God is looking for them, and when he did not see them He calls out the man, "Adam, where are you?" From the brush, Adam responds to God, "I was naked. I was scared. [And] I hid."

God says, "Wait a minute! Who told you that you were naked? Did you eat the fruit?"

Adam says, "This woman you gave me." God asked the woman and she said the serpent deceived me. Then God hands out the curses to the serpent, the woman, and the man; and though all of them have some deep theological, spiritual, social, and economic connotations it is what he said to the woman that arrests our attention in the life of Savannah. Here it is in verse 16 of the 3rd chapter of Genesis: To the woman he said, "I will greatly increase your pangs in childbearing; in pain you shall bring forth children, yet your desire shall be for your husband, And he shall rule over you." There it is in plain letters: the Curse of Eve is that she will have pain in childbirth, that her desire will be for her man and that her husband will rule over her. In The Message it says that last part of verse 16 like this: "You'll want to please your husband, but he'll lord it over you."

I must admit that upon reading this I felt unqualified to treat this text that pronounces judgment on a woman. Please don't misunderstand me. I do understand that in the Western societal training of my patriarchal male-dominated machismo lens I should be able to agree quickly with such a judgment. However, when you infuse the grace of a loving God, coupled with the fact that Eve was not by herself, and finally add the deep Egalitarian subscription that I strive to have as it pertains to a commitment to Kingdom Quality, and as I attempt to defeat the traditional and sometimes limiting views that I was raised on concerning the issues of women and men, I had to realize that I had a problematic lens pertaining to my exegesis of this text.

I felt underqualified as it pertains to the lens of the womanist theory and the Curse of Eve, so I engaged the counsel of three generations of womanist scholars to understand and proclaim to you today. I talked to a new scholar, Dr. Kimberly Johnson, who was then a professor in the communications department of Xavier University in New Orleans. I got weigh in from Dr. Renita Weems, dean of academic affairs at American Baptist College. And I called Dr. Valerie Bridgeman, a tenured professor in preaching at Lancaster Theological Seminary. I called them because I needed some scholars who happened to be female to weigh in on what seemed to be an unfair, sexist, and chauvinistic judgment by the Lord. But these sisters weighed in to help me understand.

Dr. Kim Johnson said that she would argue that the sister, though seemingly having it all, lacks the most important component: she has not really learned how to love herself. Dr. Johnson suggests that this is seen throughout society and is especially prevalent among young African American woman who are on the grind who are disproportionately outpacing their male counterparts. She asserts that it is never a competition about who has what or what status has been achieved as long as the sister on whatever level and with whichever man knows how to love herself. Without that, the person ends up like Savannah, willing to have any man even if she has to settle for someone else's man. Loving yourself is definitely a way to handle the curse of Eve.

Dr. Renita Weems suggests that this judgment of the Lord reveals a truth that most people don't really like to admit: that women are sexual creatures and enjoy it. The lens of male-dominated culture and the august ego affixed to it does not have room for a woman who is comfortable with her sexuality. As a result, many times women have to hide their desires so as not to seem too sexual. The other side to this, Dr. Weems said, is that the woman is most powerful in the desire stage of this interaction because when interaction become intercourse it will ultimately strengthen the man while weakening the woman for that man. The transference of power from the interaction stage to the intercourse stage is the essence of the power that men have to lord over women. The power originates in the women; however, it is often not taken but given away. When women give their power away they experience the curse of Eve.

Dr. Valerie Bridgeman says that this curse of Eve is descriptive in a spiritual sense of what happens when the covenant is broken between a woman and her God. I will admit that I had trouble seeing this view at first because of my patriarchal lens. It is in that lens that whether we were taught it or not many of us assumed that it was Adam who embodied Eve's relationship with God. Dr. Valerie shared with me a revelation that transcended the way I see the creation narrative. Many believe, I'm paraphrasing, that it was Adam who was the go-between of God and woman; however, she said they already had a relationship. We know this because God made and built her while Adam was asleep, which means God and Eve had a relationship while Adam was still snoring. The curse of Eve comes whenever a woman breaks her covenant with her God and replaces it with a man.

The Bible, as it always does, gives us some hope for any sister who is dealing with the curse of Eve. There is hope for any single woman or wife who finds they are struggling with either of these viewpoints. The assurance of God's grace comes in the first part of what has been called the curse of Eve. God says to Eve, "I will great increase your pain in childbearing and through pain you shall bring forth children." There it is. This is to me is the liberation and celebration of any sister who has ever been a victim of the curse of Eve. This is what can bring meaning to the profound pain that some relationships can cause for both men and women, but in this case especially women. God has called you to produce and give life even through the pain. There have to be some sisters reading this who can get on the phone and/or the internet and encourage a sister. Tell her, "I know it hurt, but keep producing."

11
Waiting to Exhale: Robin and the Painful Past

by Zedric K. Clayton, II
Senior Pastor of The City of Truth, Clarksdale, Mississippi

The woman said to him, "Sir, give me this water so that I won't get thirsty and have to keep coming here to draw water." He told her, "Go, call your husband and come back." "I have no husband," she replied. Jesus said to her, "You are right when you say you have no husband. The fact is, you have had five husbands, and the man you now have is not your husband. What you have just said is quite true" (John 4:15-18, NIV).

It had been a long day of work filled with meetings, presentations, and planning. All of this was being done in preparation for her next big project. Maybe it was due to the stress and anxiety of the day, or perhaps it was just out of habit, but Robin Stokes, a young, beautiful, high-powered corporate executive, decides that she does not want to be home alone for the night. So she invites Michael, her overly eager, highly interested, short and chubby coworker over for a midnight rendezvous. We don't have to wonder for long about her motives for doing so; in fact, her testimony removes all ambiguity when she says she "needed to feel a man."

You see, the back-story is that she had just broken up with her boyfriend of two years, Russell. In fact, she would be with Russell tonight if she had her druthers. She loved Russell. With Russell she had fun, with Russell she made love and had built up an appetite for intimacy, but with Russell she also had heartbreak and cheating . . . so tonight she calls Michael. Even though he is not a man she loves, and even though she does not really care about him and is not even attracted to him, she calls over Michael.

The truth is Robin has no desire of a connection with him beyond this night. She called him over ONLY because she knew he would come and she just needed to feel the touch of a man. In other words she just wants sex. Robin reveals to us that she had reached a point where she just wanted a need met. She says, "He's no Russell, but I guess he will have to do." Therefore, it comes without surprise that after sex, as he is smiling with satisfaction and fulfillment, she is both unfulfilled and unsatisfied. Amazingly, however, in this unfulfilled and unsatisfied moment they begin to have a conversation about her fantasies.

Robin begins to confess that she wants a house in suburbs, two or three children, marriage and a family. Michael affirms that some of those things he already has and whatever he does not have they could get together. He says to her, "I can give you that and more." It is at that moment that she tells him to kiss her softly and then it happens—she exhales. Upon her exhaling one would predict that Robin is going to fall in love with Michael and live happily ever after. However, Robin exhales and says to herself, "He almost feels like the real thing."

You see, Michael for her was a placeholder because her heart and her mind is somewhere else and with someone else. It is important to note that this is not the first time that she has done this. There have been lots of men she has slept with and had no emotional attachment to. Time and time again she has allowed men to use her and abuse her. Over and over she has given her body to men, who fell drastically short of the standard she really wanted and deserved, so that she could feel the touch of a man.

The question becomes then, how did she get this way? She has a lot going for herself: she's beautiful, successful, and smart, and she has her own house, her own car, and her own money. In essence, she is what some hip hoppers call "a 5-star chick." The question, though, still remains: What pushed her to live like this?

One day while at the pool with Savannah, Robin tells her story in third person. She confesses that she once was dating a married man who was promising her he was going to leave his wife to be with her. So she quit her job and moved to the city in which he lived. Shortly after she found out that she was three months pregnant with his baby. She declares that he ended up dumping her, saying that his kids would be too hurt if he left. As a result she had an abortion and revealed that she never told a soul, not even her mother. Robin professes/confesses that because of this, she "never looked at men quite the same again." It is with this statement alone that Robin exposes that she is still held captive by the pain of her past experience. This secret has haunted her and caused her to live a life of shame and regret. Robin, like many of us in here today, has a past that hurt, that has left her scarred, that has stunted her growth, and that has negatively shaped her view of love and intimacy.

My friends, I want to suggest that Robin is not the only one who is suffering with a painful past, for such is the case for the woman in our text. She was considered to be an around-the-way girl. She was born with two strikes against her—one, because she was a woman and two, because she was a Samaritan. If that was not enough she picked up a bad reputation. I mean, she was not thought to be a good, clean Christian girl. No, she was one of the girls in the community whom none of the mothers wanted their son to marry. In fact, she had been labeled as the outcast of the community.

She really didn't have too many friends because you know the saying is birds of a feather flock together, and the other "proper" women didn't want to be known for her type of feather. Her name was always on the gossip line and her business was all in the street. Every time she would appear in public, people would whisper and point as she walked by. She had low self-esteem because no one would openly show her love. She was the cousin whom no one in the family wanted to claim. She stopped coming to the family reunions because she just did not feel like being looked down on by the people who were supposed to love her.

She was the daughter whom her parents really didn't talk about. At her parents' house, her picture was hidden, although there were multiple pictures of her brothers and sisters out for all to see. She was the black sheep of the family. She was the child about whom her parents wondered: Where did we go wrong with her? And on top of all of that, all her life she was taught that she was not worth much because she was a woman and a Samaritan.

Every man she met in her life used her for what she had and left. They would call her to come over late at night when everyone was asleep so they could have a little fun with her. But the next morning they wouldn't say two words to her, and what she did the night before would be known to all the people because the man from the night before would go and discuss how she was with his friends. Every Jew she encountered looked down on her because of where she was from. These events left her hurt and scarred. They left her with present residue of her past experiences.

Jesus and his disciples left Judea to go to Galilee. He was leaving because the Pharisees were keeping score of baptisms, making it seem as if Jesus and John were competing against each other. While on that journey, Jesus got tired and rested at Jacob's well. He sent the disciples to get some food for lunch. And the woman of Samaria came to the well where Jesus was sitting and began to draw water out of the well.

While there, Jesus asked the woman for a drink. Immediately she got an attitude with Jesus because he was a Jew and she was a Samaritan and because he was a man and she was a woman. She got an attitude with him. She could not believe Jesus would talk to her because all of the Jews, especially the men of her past, looked down on her. Because of her painful past experiences she could not believe that this Jewish man would think enough of her to have a conversation with her. Due to the pain of her past, she is convinced that what she is experiencing is the best that life has to offer.

It is not hard for many of us to understand this feeling. In a real sense, the feeling of our present being paralyzed by the various pains of our past is the feeling that many of us live with and battle against every day. We deal with some past family hurt, a failed marriage, the loss of a loved one, a child who went astray, past addiction, some tragedy from college, or some past church drama. There are things that have happened to us and we have yet to get over them. The text is tailored to teach us that when these things go left unresolved it makes us act out in three different ways.

The first way that we act out when we have unresolved issues is we lose trust in people.

Jesus asks her for a drink and she thinks that he is trying to run game on her because he came to the well with no bucket. Everybody knows that if you are coming to the well to get water you are supposed to bring a bucket. But here is this man claiming that all he wants is a drink of water but has nothing to dip the water out of the well with. Scholars have said that the well was the place the men in the community would come to find women. So when Jesus asks her for water she was probably saying to herself, "Sir, I have heard that tired line before. I am not going to fall for that anymore."

She automatically thought that Jesus was like all the other men she has met at this well. She had her guard up because so many other men have hurt her until she feels that all men are the same.

This too sounds like Robin, who has begun to live life in a way that she tries never to be hurt by a man again. Because of the pain she endured in her past relationship, she protects her heart by convincing herself that all men are dogs. Her view and image of men in general has been altered because of the mistakes of one man. She has lost respect for the entire male species because of the hurt that she has suffered. She has trust issues. Brothers and sisters, if we decide to be truthful, some us have trust issues. We feel that everyone is out to get us. We walk through life always second-guessing the motives of other people. We say things like, "Why are you being so nice? Why are you always smiling at me? Why are you buying this for me? Why are you complimenting me?" We feel that every kind gesture, every conversation has a hidden agenda. As a result, we walk around angry so that no one will get close to us.

We walk around with an attitude all the time because we are trying to stop people from getting close to us. We declare, "If they think I'm mean then they won't try to get in my personal space. And if they do not get in my personal space they cannot hurt me." We sabotage good relationships. The relationship could be going well but we sit around looking for bad. We try to make every issue bigger than it really is until either they decide to leave us or we convince ourselves to leave them. Because of the pain of our past we rob ourselves of the privilege of simply being happy and whole.

The second way that we act out when we have unresolved issues is we search for an escape.

This woman was trying her best daily to avoid the people of her community. She would not go out in public unless it was extremely necessary. She was trying to find ways to hide from the realities of life. This is seen in the blatant examples of her breaking the normal routine of most Samaritan woman. First she stopped coming to the well in the morning when most of the women would come because she felt that she would be the talk of the morning at best or at worst, the women would treat her as if she was dirty and would look down on her because of her past. She would rather come out during the hottest hour of the day than to have to face the women of the community. But that was not really working for her because her desire was to never come back to the well. Look at the text in verse 15: she told Jesus to give her living water so that she would never have to come back to the well. She wanted Jesus to help her hide from life. She wanted to lock herself in her house to never be seen again.

Robin also searches for escapes. Her biggest escape is sex. She no longer sees it as a sign of intimacy and love shared with someone special. She views it as a method by which she can get what she wants from a man. But not only that, she also sees sex as a way to forget about the problems that she is dealing with in her life, if only for a moment. As a result, she jumps from bed to bed laying with men whom she no longer sees as human but rather as a means by which she receives relief, because the hurt in her life is so severe that she needed away to release it. So she allowed men to get close enough to get her body while keeping her broken heart under lock and key, all because she needed a momentary vacation from the reality of her pain.

This is not far from the shore of some of the souls that are listening to this right now. Some of us are either hiding or we know people who are hiding from life. These types of people dread coming to church because the people of that community know their past and have even used their past against them. The church won't allow them to serve because of their past. So these people resent coming to worship; they come late and leave early on Sunday so they won't have to deal with the hypocritical looks of church folk. The only reason they keep coming is because they know God requires them to come, but at the same time they are looking for any type of excuse not to come back.

Some folk are hiding on their job. They call off any chance they get because they are running from the people on their job that know their business. And when they do go to work they avoid people all day so that they won't have to face the criticism of the people on the job. The only reason they don't quit is because they need the money. Believe it or not some are hiding from home. They do whatever they cannot to go home. They are looking for any reason they can to stay out longer. That's why they get two and three jobs, not because they love working or not because they need the money, but because they just hate going home. Some find any reason to stay at church; they are here every day just hanging around because they just don't want to go home. Because at home, a husband is constantly reminded by his wife of the ONE time he tipped out on the family. Or a wife is constantly reminded by her husband of the fact that for years the child that he thought was his turned out to belong to someone else. A daughter is constantly reminded of the time she was caught with a boy in the house. A son is repeatedly reminded of the time his mother found a dime bag of weed in his pocket when she was washing his clothes. So to avoid the reminder, they choose to escape.

The third way we act out is we begin to punish the new people in our life for the stuff the old folk in our life did to us.

The Bible says that she had been married five times and the guy she was living with now was not even her husband. This means that five times in her life she walked down the aisle to give her hand in marriage to five different people, and all five times they left her. She had been told five times in her life that she was the one for five different people. She had been promised five times by five different men that they were going to love her "'til death did them part," but five times that promise had been broken. She was known as the wife of and associated to five different men. Her heart had been broken five times by men who said they loved her but called a quits on the marriage.

So this new man in her life didn't even have a fighting chance. She told him: It's alright to sleep with me, it's alright to live in the same house as me and sleep in the same bed as me, it's alright for us to have kids together, it's alright for us to look like we are married and have the benefits of married people, but I don't want your last name and I don't want to give you my hand in marriage because I know you are going to leave me sooner or later just like the five men before. So if I don't have your last name and if I don't have your ring on my finger maybe it won't hurt as bad when you walk out on me and the kids. Because I just can't go through the pain of my husband leaving me anymore; it's too emotionally draining and I can't take it anymore. So she punishes her new man for the stuff the old men in her life did to her.

In the case of Robin, she rejected Michael, a guy who really cared for her and who wanted to fulfill her every desire, a man who at least showed that she meant a lot more just a person to have late-night fun with. However, she rejected the possibility of being happy with him because of the place in which her past has forced her. Robin was never going to give Michael a chance, not because he was a bad person, not because he proved to be disrespectful to her, but rather because she chose to punish him for something he didn't have anything to do with. She refused to believe that something good could actually happen to her. In her mind a man who was genuine did not exist. Therefore, she rejected Michael.

Friends, some of us today are doing this same thing, aren't we? You can't fully love your husband because you are punishing him because of the man who broke your heart in high school. You can't let your wife know the real you because you are punishing her for the girl who took advantage of your emotions years ago. You won't allow your younger daughter to go out and be a young person because her older sister got pregnant in high school. You can't fully love your son because he reminds you of his father who used you and left. You can't love your daughter because every time you see her you see her father, the man who took advantage of you in college. It's because we are still dealing with the residue of our painful past. But let me encourage you. Though we may have a painful past, the blessing is that it is our past and we serve a God of another chance. Even though we may have been hurt, God always grants another chance to reclaim our joy, our faith, our dignity, and our selves.

For Robin, this occurred when she found out that she was pregnant again, this time by Russell. Yet instead of aborting the baby like she had done previously in her life, she decided to change her actions to prepare herself for motherhood. For her, this meant dumping the man but keeping the baby. She chose to love herself and the life of her unborn child over the pleasure that came from her dead-end relationship with Russell.

For the woman at the well, deliverance showed at the place of her deepest pain, the well. She was punishing the 6th man in her life because of the stuff the five men before him did to her. But she came in contact with a seventh man, who knew everything about her but still loved her. This seventh man understood how messed up she really was, but it didn't matter to him. This seventh man did not care how much she messed up or how much she failed; he still desired relationship with her. This seventh man came to complete her, to fix the broken pieces in her life. The blessing today is that this same man desires to help us as well.

He wants to give us back our joy, our faith, and our love. He wants us to smile again, hope again, and dream again. Who is this man? His name is Jesus, the Lily of valley! Jesus, the bright and morning star! Jesus, our joy in sorrow! Jesus, our hope for tomorrow! The same Jesus, that one Friday evening, went to a hill called Calvary and died for our sins. But the record is that he didn't stay dead, but he got up from the grave. And because he got up, we can get up from the pains of our past.

12

Waiting to Exhale: Bernadine and the Love Hangover

The Torment of Separation

"I have come into my garden, my sister, my bride;
I have gathered my myrrh along with my balsam.
I have eaten my honeycomb and my honey;
I have drunk my wine and my milk.
Eat, friends;
Drink and imbibe deeply, O lovers."

"I was asleep but my heart was awake.
A voice! My beloved was knocking:
'Open to me, my sister, my darling,
My dove, my perfect one!
For my head is drenched with dew,
My locks with the damp of the night.'
"I have taken off my dress,
How can I put it on again?
I have washed my feet,
How can I dirty them again?
"My beloved extended his hand through the opening,
And my feelings were aroused for him.

"I arose to open to my beloved;
And my hands dripped with myrrh,
And my fingers with liquid myrrh,
On the handles of the bolt.
"I opened to my beloved,
But my beloved had turned away and had gone!
My heart went out to him as he spoke.
I searched for him but I did not find him;
I called him but he did not answer me.
"The watchmen who make the rounds in the city
          found me,
They struck me and wounded me;
The guardsmen of the walls took away my shawl from me.
"I adjure you, O daughters of Jerusalem,
If you find my beloved,
As to what you will tell him:
For I am lovesick" (Song of Solomon 5:1-8, NASB).

I call it the Gibson Challenge, and any couples that I have married
know it well. It is a sacrificial rite of passage that I issue to all of my
premarital couples. You see, after about four months of counseling,
ending a month before the wedding, I challenge the couple concerning the responsibility of their physical intimacy and their sexual life.
I don't ask them to commit to not having any sexual, physical intimacy for the last month before the wedding. Instead, I suggest that
they fast together and develop the spiritual and social ties of marriage, as the sexual tie is the easiest and will be there. Finally, I promise them that if they do this, their marital night or whenever they con-
summate will be not only awesome but also blessed.

I know that we are saved and sanctified but indeed we are also
sexual, and when one thinks of the evening of a wedding one does
not think of hymns and anthems. In fact, personally, when it comes

to the wedding evening, I don't think of anything churchy; not praise and worship, not prayer, and not even a choir selection. Nothing churchy! Well, I take that back; I do think of the welcome and the offering, but you will get that on the way home. I'm just saying, you expect the wedding night to have a different anointing than church.

You are hoping for the gift of love-laced passion, engrossed with a heat that will consume you but not burn you. I believe that this is in some way ensured to the couples I counsel, if they are unselfish enough to accept the Gibson Challenge and sacrifice for a month before their wedding night. Pledging to give themselves to God instead of each other ensures a night of blessed awesomeness.

In part I believe that in the text, this is what the woman was anticipating as she lay there on their marital bed on this night described by her. She is excited because Jewish tradition was much tougher than the Gibson Challenge, for it called for more than a month of sacrifice from the engaged when it came to sexual matters—you had to wait a whole year. In fact, this was such a common belief in the Ancient Near Eastern Cultures that you will remember even Esther was made to wait a whole year before she was granted "one night with the king [of Persia]."

This woman, whom many believe to be the Queen of Sheba, has possibly waited a whole year for this night, this night with the one whom she calls her Beloved. I have a long way to go, but let me put this piece on front street: if they were willing to wait and exercise discipline in order that they might experience a night of special physical and sexual activity, what does that say about us and our declination of morals? You see, the sad truth of the matter is that our society has descended into the deep and dark chasm of selfishness and objectivity. Unlike the society in the text, one that will wait for up to a whole year so that they might offer themselves to another as one as worthy, we don't concentrate on the worth of who we are and what we have to offer. We much rather objectify each other and see what we can get for little or no commitment.

The woman waited and prepared herself for possibly up to a year, and this was the night that she was to present herself to her man, wholly and acceptable. Now I must tell you that this text that I have picked for you is possibly one of the most sexually charged passages in all of the Holy Writ. It is filled with all types of euphemisms, light allegorical and metaphorical statements. This should not be foreign to us because the English language is full of them, and culturally we use them all of the time. For instance, to say that someone "passed away" is a euphemism for he died, or if someone is "under the weather" we know that is a euphemism for her being sick. This passage also contains the use of double entendre, statements that lift images that have two different or hidden meanings, like the slaves singing "Steal Away to Jesus," which meant to sneak away to have church as well as the possibility of the Underground Railroad coming through.

There are euphemisms and double entendre in this text, many of which have an erotic leaning. Let us pick it up in verse two where it says: "I have come into my garden, my sister, my bride; I have gathered my myrrh along with my balsam. I have eaten my honeycomb and my honey; I have drunk my wine and my milk. Eat, friends; Drink and imbibe deeply, O lovers." "I was asleep but my heart was awake."

Verse one is most likely the toast of the groom at the wedding reception. He begins to speak to the potential of the richness, sweetness, and production of his equal, his wife. He speaks of myrrh, which was a perfumed oil and honey from a honeycomb, which was tasty, and he speaks of wine and milk. Milk dealt with the ability to produce and sustain life while wine was festive and denoted prosperity as well as lowered the inhibitions.

Then the voice shifts to the woman who is now waiting for him at the home, and she says "I was asleep but my heart was awake."

She says I am waiting for him to come home, so I am kind of asleep but my mind is awake and I am listening for the sound of my lover. This is when we get deep into the poetic language. The text says that this lady says: "A voice! My beloved was knocking: 'Open to me, my sister, my darling, my dove, and my perfect one! For my head is drenched with dew, My locks with the damp of the night.' "I have taken off my dress, How can I put it on again? I have washed my feet, how can I dirty them again? My beloved extended his hand through the opening."

You will note that the word "knocking" here in Hebrew carries the connotation of nudging or pushing. He is nudging her and says My Darling Dove, Perfect One. He is laying it on thick and says, Baby my head is drenched with dew and my locks are damp. He means, Baby, I have been working hard and my hair is drenched. She says in a teasing and flirtatious way, I have taken off my dress, my undergarment, and washed my feet. In the Hebrew feet and hands are a metaphor for genitalia, like when the Bible says that Ruth covers the feet of Boaz. She says I have cleaned up my "feet" for you, do you want me to get dirty? And then she says he extended his hand through the opening that she opened for him. Again, this is the wedding night, a night that they had waited for, for at least a year. Her testimony was that her heart or body was thrilled. In fact everything within her was blessed. How do I know? I know this because the King James Version says that her bowels or the core of who she was were moved for him and the inference was "And I was his."

In fact, if you keep reading it says in verses 5–6 that on the same night or sometime later she went to open herself again; after she had once again anointed herself with perfume and was once again presentable, she offered. But this time, after the marital bed was consummated and after some time together, he is nowhere to be found. In fact, she slips on something to go and find him, but she says that she cannot find him, and even worse than that, the watchmen of the city now treat her disrespectfully. In fact, there is even an allusion to them raping and beating her.

This is significant because this is the type of treatment that men would give a harlot, not someone's wife. But the question is, was she a wife or has she been left in a cold way by her husband basically with no warning, on or sometime after the wedding night and after a mind-blowing climax? From the pages we hear her testimony to the daughters of Jerusalem, "If you see my Beloved, tell him that I am lovesick."

She's says I'm lovesick and brokenhearted. I have heartache, agony of the mind, a bleeding heart, I'm crushed, in misery, I'm depressed, I'm bitter, and I have a heavy heart. She is grieving, is downright hurt, and has what Bernadine Harris calls a Love Hangover. This is what she called it as she takes most of her husband's clothes, put them in the white BMW 7 series, and burns them in their driveway, only then taking the rest of his things and selling them for a dollar apiece in the Love Hangover yard sale.

Let me hasten to say, like the lady in the text, she had no idea it would end up like this, especially not for her. I mean, her wedding night was much different than that of the sister in the text. In fact, they didn't have much—all they really had was love and, of course, student loan debt. But none of that mattered because she and John were going to make it. He had a dream of them owning their own business and that they would be wealthy, and though she herself had a masters degree and had the dream of owning her own catering business, she put her aspirations on pause so that she might help him. She became his administrative assistant at work, doing the menial tasks of making the business work, opening up to him, for him, and with him; letting him take the best of her body, her mind, her energy, and her creativity. After all it was for them; she was doing this for the team. She is singing background for the team while hiding her solo voice for the big picture.

Then the kids came. No real need for her to work or start a business. She decided consciously or subconsciously that this way, his
way, is better. After all, she thought, the kids need me and he needs
me. I will open myself to them and give to them: school meetings,
practice, business function after business function, organizing the
day to day of the house, colds, sickness, and sex when he wants to,
and even when she doesn't, she still does.

She continually opens herself like she is doing on this New Year's
Eve night, the same New Year's Eve that her friend Savannah who
just moved to Phoenix from Denver was about to meet Lionel,
who showed up with another date, and experience the Curse of
Eve. The night that her friend Robin was sitting at home without
a date due to her Painful Past, she, Bernadine was once again
preparing for a party to which she did not want to go. Though she
had been in this place before this was like no other night, for on
this night as she is opening herself up once again for her beloved
John, he tells her that not only is he having an affair but he does
not want to be with her any longer.

After 11 years of marriage, two children, building a life and a
company together, he leaves? After 11 years of doing whatever he
said, growing her hair and putting off her dreams, he's leaving? Her
thoughts are pronounced, I have an MBA that I put on hold and
you are going to leave me all of a sudden? She, like the woman in
the text, is devastated, broken, crushed, and knows not what to do.
By the time Savannah shows up to see her it's more than apparent
that she has been crying, has not cleaned up, and is sitting there
watching the wedding and anniversary tapes. She is mad not only
at him but also at herself because in her words, "I had no plan B!"

But who was she kidding? She knew this was not all of a sudden.
She had been lying to herself. Because they had all that she wanted, their finances were tight. She had given her power away and
forfeited her identity for her man. She had chosen to give herself
away and has absolutely nothing left. She has no reward for the

time and no loyalty for opening herself so wide. If that was not enough she has to admit that she knew that he had been cheating for a long time but covered it up. After all of that he is in no way repentant and he decides not only to leave but also to leave her and the children with nothing. She, in his mind, was to get no share of the millions that they have earned, none of property he has purchased, no ownership in the company that they have labored for together, not even full custody of the children. He left her with nothing except a love hangover, and she loses it! She burns his clothes and his car and sells all of his stuff for a dollar. She cuts her hair and begins to frequent clubs, and the woman she hated and feared for taking her husband is the exact woman she is becoming. She is experiencing what is called moral meltdown and fatigue.

Most men don't know much about this, but I guarantee the ladies do. Moral meltdown and fatigue is when doing right repeatedly turns out bad for you and you end up hurt. You are nice and he still hurts you; you are faithful and he cheats. You tell the truth but he lies; you are considerate but you are taken for granted. Time and time again you do right and it seemingly only gets you hurt. You reach the point of moral fatigue and you begin to question morally is it worth it? Furthermore, you wonder what it would be like to be bad just one time.

Bernadine did this; she became willing to be the other woman to a married man, the enemy to love and marriage, justifying that by saying, "I tapped danced for him [John] for 11 years, I was his white woman for 11 years, I'll be damned if I get a new owner; but I do need to feel someone even if it is a lie." All of this is because, in the words of the woman in the text, she is lovesick. Or, in Bernadine's vernacular, she has a love hangover.

Her choice of words, love hangover, really messed me up, because for those of us who have not always lived super-holy, and for those of us who need prayer on a day to day, the word hangover has a universal image and connotation. A hangover deals of course with when, after a night of hanging out and ingesting too much alcohol for your body to properly process and excrete, you experience adverse after-effects to the chemical reaction of the alcohol that "hangover" into the next day. When you have an overload of the chemicals in alcohol and it is more than the body can handle, process, and digest, then it will leave some after-effects that hangover, and there are symptoms of that due to the chemical imbalance created.

This, however, would mean nothing had it not been for a biological field of study that started in 1976 that argues that at the physiological level, not mental and emotional, love at best is a chemical reaction. The study argues this premise on the following basis: that love, like all things bound to the universe, is nonexistent without some amount of physics and chemistry attached to it. As a scientist cynically pointed out, cupid's arrows would never have been effective if they had not been first dipped in one unromantically named chemical phenethylamine. Nor would the human body's reaction have given us dramas like Romeo and Juliet, if oxytocin did not have its way, for together these two form the chemistry of love.

In a real sense, it is phenethylamine that is known as the "love molecule". It is released when the eyes see something that it likes. It is secreted, if you will, when the hands are touched in an affirming and enticing way. It produces as its side effects sweaty palms, shakiness, nervousness, and restlessness. This chemical is present in chocolate, and in regular doses it is acceptable. However, if ingested in a manner that would be considered an overdose, its side effects can be heavy breathing, racing and erratic impulses, and heady emotion.

Oxytocin, on the other hand, is the chemical that is known as the cuddling or intimate hormone. This promotes the need to be physically held and satisfies the desire for intimacy. These are also called endorphins and they are released the strongest during climax. It is during orgasm that oxytocin does its best work, producing feelings of contentment, reduced anxiety and fear, an increase in trust, and a sense of security.

Together they do not induce a giddy high alone, but one that is coupled with calmness and stability, hence one of the reasons why people stay married. The longer they are married, the longer two people usually stay together because this chemical is addictive and builds tolerance. It is the endorphins that trigger grief on a spouse's death, long separation, or divorce. It produces those uncontrollable yearnings for togetherness; endorphins produce a love hangover.

I dare say that if all of us are truthful we can look back over our lives and find moments that we were guilty of having a love hangover. Let down by life and love, we have all found ourselves in a place where a breakup caught us while we were thinking that things were good at best and, at the least, salvageable. And finding that we are not where we want to be and definitely not where we used to be, but inside longing to feel like we used to feel, we find ourselves suffering from a love hangover. The love that we were used to has been taken away from us and leaves us in a state of deficiency. I'm sick because what I had gotten used to is no more. The chemical reaction to the mix of physical, emotional, and mental stimuli has produced an overdose of emotions that, for whatever reason, can no longer be sustained and the longing for what had become normal produces a hangover.

Again this terminology, concept, and scenario are most likely associated with the consumption of alcohol, and it is to this metaphor that we will look in order to find its remedy. For an alcohol hangover there are many suggested remedies. The one that is touted as the best is also the simplest; it is called a Bloody Mary. This is a drink that gives you both alcohol and nutrients. It gave you some of the stuff that made you sick as well as some things that will build you. It replaces what was taken from you and then gives you more than you had before the infraction. So if I have a love hangover, I need some love that can give to me without taking away from me.

Bernadine found this in James, a lawyer who was in town on business. She is at her lowest, but in one night of intimate non-sexual exchange he repairs, restores, and even redeems her belief in love. He gave her a love that she did not have to work for, a love that she did not have to earn. He shared with her a love that she could experience and not leave empty; it was a love that did not cost here anything. It was through this love that she was able to shake her hangover, and it was while reading a letter from him that she was finally able to do it; she exhaled.

Oh, I wish I had somebody who has ever been beat down by love. You were so beat down by love that you were almost ready to quit, but your testimony is that God did not send you a James but he sent you Jesus. Jesus came down through forty and two generations and gave you what you had lost and more. Talk to your neighbor and say, in the words of the old hymn, "love lifted me, love lifted me, when nothing else could help—love lifted me!" He got rid of my hangover!

13

Waiting to Exhale: Gloria and the Crisis of Co-dependency

She said to her son Jacob, "Listen. I overheard your father say to Esau, 'Bring me some wild game and prepare me a delicious meal. Then I will bless you in the Lord's presence before I die.' Now, my son, listen to me. Do exactly as I tell you. Go out to the flocks, and bring me two fine young goats. I'll use them to prepare your father's favorite dish. Then take the food to your father so he can eat it and bless you before he dies." "But look," Jacob replied to Rebekah, "my brother, Esau, is a hairy man, and my skin is smooth. What if my father touches me? He'll see that I'm trying to trick him, and then he'll curse me instead of blessing me." But his mother replied, "Then let the curse fall on me, my son! Just do what I tell you. Go out and get the goats for me" (Genesis 27:6-13, NLT)!

"Our time begins now," I said to her as she nervously walked into the office. "Rebekah, I want you to feel comfortable and to know that for the next 50 minutes that you can talk to me about whatever you want. We can discuss your childhood, your parents, young adult life, marriage, children, even your relationship with God. Just know that when the 50 minutes ends, your session ends. Where would you like to start, with the good times or with the bad times?"

She took a deep breath and said, "I think I would like to start with when it got bad because everything to that point seemed pretty OK. I guess I can trace the trouble to that morning that I took the early pregnancy test. You see, this was a major potential celebration, because though we have been married for 20 years, and had been trying, we never had any kids. This hurt because I could hear the gossip of the people in the neighborhood, some of them friends, saying that I was barren because God was upset with me.

"We were excited on that day when I saw the plus sign and not a minus. I ran and told Isaac. Needless to say, he was overjoyed; we were fully excited. In fact, we thought that we could not possibly be any happier. That was until the day of our scheduled ultrasound and they told us that they saw two heartbeats instead of one. We were expecting two boys and not one. Twins!"

"Isn't it just like God to take you from nothing to more than you can handle in one moment? You see, my husband prayed for me and there is just something about prayer. But I think that may have been when it started. While Isaac was busy handing out cigars that said it's a boy, of course he bought double the amount to make sure he could tell everyone to take two. He was reminding everyone how virile and manly he was because he had sired two male offspring, while I was silently struggling with both emotional and physical pain."

"While he went out and drank beer with the boys, I was at home struggling with swollen feet, morning sickness, and abdominal pain. Though I do understand that I was an emotional wreck, taking him on a roller coaster of emotional highs one moment and lows the next, it hurt that he was preoccupied with his part of the arrangement so much so that he didn't notice that it produced an emotional and mental separation that was more painful than the pain I was experiencing physically."

"In fact, I know that it's supposed to be uncomfortable when the baby stretches, kicks, and flips, but I was experiencing something that even the doctors had never seen, nor could they explain. I realized at that point that my pain was something that only God could handle. So I went to my husband because he is usually the one who goes to God for me, and of course though he was physically there, he was mentally absent. So I decided that I would go to God for myself; it's good to have a personal relationship with God."

"I asked God why was I in so much pain? I mean, after all these years you finally give me a baby and now the pain. God said that there was a war going on in my womb, a battle in the midst of my bowels. Literally, God said that I was pregnant with twins who represented two nations. God said that one would be stronger than the other but that the eldest would serve the youngest. This was heavy, but I understood and I struggled for the rest of the pregnancy. Isaac didn't notice."

"When the babies were born, I must admit that though I should have been happy, I secretly held a grudge. I had an emotional resentment against Isaac, resentment that came from unresolved pain because he seemingly left me when I needed him the most. I had not felt this lonely and abandoned since my father died. The resentment quickly manifested itself too. As soon as he lifted the firstborn Esau with pride, it was then in my heart that I chose Jacob. Don't get me wrong, they were both beautiful boys. Esau was the firstborn. We named him that because he was a red boy who was also very hairy. He was not only a handsome boy—they both were—but he was strong. He was a father's dream: he was tough, he liked to fight, he was a good hunter, and he liked to eat game."

"But his brother, my Jacob, was a milder softer boy. He didn't like to fight and that was OK. He was the thinker. He wasn't into playing outside and being tough and rough. Most of all he was mine. Not much changed around the house as they grew up. Isaac had Esau and I had Jacob. Isaac and Esau would go the field, and my Jacob and I would stay in the house. They would go hunt and we would prepare to cook when they got back. Isaac and Esau shared hobbies, while my Jacob and I shared conversation. Isaac taught his son everything he knew, and I taught my Jacob everything as well."

"Then things came to a head. It was when I heard Isaac telling Esau that he was ready to give him the Blessing. Of course, you know the blessing was the final passing of the mantle or the laying of hands from the father to his eldest son. If the father had any favor, the blessing was his to give to his oldest son."

"That," Rebekah said, "is when I knew I had to do something. I called my Jacob and began to tell him the plan that I had for him to steal his brother's blessing. I told him to go get me a young goat so that I could prepare it for his father. Now this was going to be tricky because Isaac was expecting some wild game to be prepared by Esau. I was going prepare that goat and I used an old near-eastern recipe. I spiced it with salt, onions, garlic, and some lemon juice, and he would not know the difference."

"Then I told Jacob that we would take the hair of the goat and put in on his neck and hands. I knew that since Isaac's vision has gotten bad, the first thing he was going to do was feel Esau to make sure that it was he. Finally, I grabbed the robe. You see, this robe had been kept in the chest in our bedroom since the boys were kids for the special blessing. Only Isaac had the key. The robe was a white garment that hung in the chest surrounded by fragrant herbs and perfumed flower; this was to keep the moths away. The robe was reserved for the firstborn, but I was willing to get this for my Jacob."

"Then Jacob said to me, 'Mom, that is enough. I am not going to do that because if I do that I might be bringing down on myself a curse instead of a blessing.' And I don't know what came over me . . . maybe it was my love for him, or maybe it was all of the time that I had invested in him. Honestly now that I think about it, it could have been my disdain because Esau got more of Isaac's attention than I did. Maybe it wasn't even about Jacob anymore. Maybe for the first time in a long time, I was doing and getting something just for me."

"When he told me about the potential of the curse I said, 'Boy, if there be a curse on you let it be on me. Just do what I say!'"

As her counselor, I must admit that when she told me that she blew me away. Although her time was now officially up I told her that I believed that I knew what was troubling her. I shared with her that I thought that through her conversation with me I could diagnose the problem. In fact, I told her that if she would just stay a little longer, I would explain to her what I thought the problem to be. I was able to do this because her case reminded me of another case that I dealt with. Of course physician/client confidentiality disallows me to disclose the name of the patient. In fact, she might be in this assembly right now. I do want you to be able identify the behavioral type, so let's just call her Gloria.

Gloria is a late thirty/early forty-something divorcee who lives in the Phoenix, Arizona, area and has a 17-year-old son we'll call Malik. Though she has friends that she can share some of her life with she struggles with a deep-seated loneliness. You see, she has not dated in a while, and though she doesn't like to admit it, she thinks she knows why. You see, she has picked up some weight and never got around to putting it down. In fact, that has been her New Year's resolution for the past several years, including this year.

By now she is down on herself and her self-esteem is low because of the weight, so she tries to cover it up with jokes. When this doesn't work she dedicates her time to trying to help others with their problems so as not to feel sorry for herself. But inside she is hurting and feels lonely. Again she hasn't had a date in a while and it's been God knows how long since intimacy. No, wait! She did tell me that when Malik's dad visited last Christmas there was that one night . . . But she said he was not that responsive and she once again felt it was because of the weight.

She has been hurt and has felt major rejection, and as a result she placed everything she had in her son, Malik. She invested all of what was and is her into her son. I mean, he was closer than a son; she depended on him to be more for her than a child. Her testimony was that he was more like the man of the house, a friend, and a companion. In fact, conversations that she should have had with other adults or conversations that she should have possibly had with her ex-husband or new love interests, she had with him.

I turned to Rebekah and said, "I said all of that to say it is my belief that you and Gloria are both dealing with codependent issues in your relationships with your sons. There are three things that I want to mention about codependence and I will let you go."

"The first thing is that codependence is the fruit of the tree of fear, which has as its core the seed of hurt. When someone is hurt physically, mentally, but more profoundly emotionally, his or her biggest fear is being hurt again. They begin to place boundaries and remove boundaries based not on merit but on the fear that was produced by hurt. It is a survival mechanism. However, when your focus is on simply surviving it drains the needed essence to have quality of life. You cannot have the freedom to truly live if you are busy holding on simply trying to survive."

"Secondly codependency stifles growth and forward progress because the fear of hurt makes you place limitations on yourself and others in order to protect yourself from the potential of being hurt. In fact, in a real sense you will limit others to keep yourself limited. Gloria would not allow Malik to go on the People to People trip to Spain. She limited him because she was scared to take a risk based on the fear of being hurt again. codependency places limits on your life that are a veiled excuse for not taking the risk of being hurt again."

"Finally, codependency happens when you invest your emotional and mental valuables in places and people that you know cannot or will not hurt or reject you. Most of the time when this is done, it places you and the other person in a dance of dysfunction. You can never be codependent by yourself. Someone has to enable the codependence and be a coconspirator in your dysfunction. They are codependent on you and you on them, and both of you are complaining the whole time. As much as you give them, they will never turn it down."

"When you do this, you place on them the unhealthy burden of being for you what you should have the courage to be for yourself. You become dependent on something or someone to give you what you should be able to give yourself. When this happens the boundaries get even more gray and unhealthy, so much so that you and the person become enmeshed."

"This is when you are hanging out with the kids instead of being a parent, or hanging out with your friends instead of being a spouse. This is when you make the son play the role of companion and not a child; calling him the man of the house when he is only 14. Or who can forget the daughter who got to take care of all of the children because she's the oldest? She knows all of your business, even things that as a kid she should not be exposed to, but she's been parentized because she's a codependent."

"It is investing in, hanging in places and with people who you think are safe for fear of being hurt again, replacing what used to be essential with something artificial. We do this all of the time with people and oftentimes even with God. In order to break codependency, one has to be willing to take the chance of sacrificing themselves as an intervention; this then allows one to love enough to let go. And, Rebekah, that is all I have been trying to say to you and the countless women in the world like you, those who have been hurt and are trying to shield themselves from future hurt by engaging in codependent behavior. In order to break that codependency, someone has to sacrifice themself as an intervention, allowing one of them to love enough to let go."

"Gloria did this by allowing Malik to go on the trip to Spain even though she said that she wouldn't. It was because she met a man we'll call Marvin. Marvin convinced her that her behavior as it pertained to Malik was overbearing and unhealthy. He put himself on the line so that she could see that if she loved Malik enough to let him go that, he, Marvin, could help her find love for herself."

I don't know about you, but that sounds strikingly familiar. While we were yet codependent and coconspirators with the enemy, there was one who loved us enough to sacrifice himself as an intervention. It was on a skull-shaped hill called Calvary that Jesus intervened and gave me enough space to know that I could love myself enough to let go of the people and the places that were preventing me from growing. Like Gloria, I ended the crisis of my codependency.

14

Love the Hurt Away

And by this we will know that we are from the truth and will reassure our hearts before him whenever our hearts condemn us; for God is greater than our hearts, and he knows everything (1 John 3:19-20, NRSV).

The stage is set and everyone is there and the judge is on the bench. The 12 jurors have nestled into the box and the bailiff has just announced the case. The stenographer has begun to type and a concerned audience of friends and family has assembled in the galley to see what will be the fate of the accused. The stage is set and it seems that everyone is there.

You are there too. You are the one on trial.

The chief prosecutor has asked if they could have a continuance to allow their special witness who had just come forth to arrive. Though the defense team has tirelessly prepared, you can see the worry on their brows, the concerned rhythm in their breathing. They look confident yet worried because of the possibility of a conviction. However, what they did not know is that the prosecution is feeling the same unsure way.

In a real sense, everything that the defense has is resting on this one witness. If this witness fails it would mean that their whole case could be lost. As your defense attorneys tell you that everything will be OK, you feel a pain in the pit of your stomach. You sit and wonder in awe about this one who supposedly has so much on you. Who could this be that has so much damning information on you? What is the identity of this person who has the power to condemn you to guilty? You are wondering this, and so is everybody there. The buzz of the conversations are growing and becoming too loud. . . . Bam! Bam! The judge slaps the gavel. "Order in the court! I said, order in the Court!"

The judge asks the prosecutor if the witness has arrived and the prosecutor looks sadly toward the door. But surprisingly he sees the investigator smiling in the affirmative with two thumbs up. Confidently the prosecutor informs the judge that the star witness against you has arrived. There is a deep breath of unbelieving anticipation heard in the room, and everyone shifts their weight to turn toward the door. Everyone wants to be the first person to see the one who can condemn you. Even you are straining your neck to see the one who has your fate in his or her hands.

As the door opens the room grows eerily quiet, and the tension is rubber band tight as the shadow of the witness is seen growing on the oak door. Then when the person comes into view there is a great gasp in the room. Even you drop your head and the prosecution smiles devilishly. Your puzzled defense attorney breaks the silence, looks at you, and says, "My God, it's you!" And that is when the harsh reality of this trial hits you like a Mack truck. It is the first time that you have to face something this deep, and that is the fact that what you know in your heart about yourself is what condemns you the most.

As you sit there on trial, you realize that it is you who is witnessing against you. No one else came forth to accuse you. No one else tried to mess you up. When you look into the witness booth it is you looking into the mirror because the only one who is there to hurt you is you. I mean, tell the truth—could anyone else do it? The answer most likely is NO, for you are the only one who knows such incriminating material. You didn't tell anyone what you had done, where you went, or how you felt. Only you could know that. You pondered that in your heart, and now it is your heart that is on the witness stand using your own information to condemn you.

Your heart is the reflection center of thought and conception as well as feeling and affection. It is the seat of love and hatred as well as the place of joy and pain. It is your heart that houses the innermost circle of humanity, where the thoughts of good and evil are conceived, and the place where mercy and condemnation reside. Your heart is the dwelling place of Christ. And it is your heart, or at least the knowledge of your heart, that is the one on the witness stand, knowing what only it knows, testifying against you.

I am sure it is a hurting feeling, a feeling of self-condemnation, when you are not happy with your own actions or outcomes and you are mad at you; a place where you blame others you know and have to face the fact that it is actually your fault.

I want to suggest that more times than not this type of hurt goes unresolved and unshared. Furthermore, it is this unresolved hurt that serves as a seed for most arguments, fractures, and breaks in our relationships. We individually have some unresolved hurts that we would rather not deal with, so we don't share it; however, when our significant other gets close to it, we get paranoid and begin to get defensive and selfish. Finally we begin to fight the very one who is there to help us.

Think about it—how do we deal with the real feeling about our unwed pregnancy, the fact that I was beloved but everyone is treating me different now? How do I face the disappointments in myself, that I did not graduate from high school and I have been fighting all of my life to rise above what Dr. Samuel DeWitt Proctor called the "scratch" (poverty) line? Can I really rebound after the embarrassing fact that I flunked out of college and lost my scholarship? How do I deal with the fact that I blew money when I had it and now I cannot even find a job and have to file bankruptcy?

How do I reconcile in my heart the reality that I am not a virgin anymore even though my parents think that I am? How can I be honest and be secure as I am struggling with homosexuality when the church I grew up in has trained my heart to condemn what feels natural to me? How can I handle being married to this abuser and worse yet forgive myself because it was me who exposed my kids to this abuser? How can I get past being raped when somehow I think it to be my fault? How do I get past the fact that I love my spouse but I hate myself for cheating? How can I get past the molestation? How do I get past the anger and regret I feel at that loved one who passed or at God for the death of my child? How do I deal with the fact that I find it hard to trust a God who supposedly makes no mistakes when it seems that He's been messing up so much with me? How do I stomach the fact that I am not who they think I am? How I deal with the fact that I have unresolved and unshared stuff?

I'll put on this façade for others to make me look good and even turn to things that make me feel good. We all have done this. We try to turn with a façade to friends and family, or to alcohol, illicit drugs, sex, pornography, gossip lines, etc. Unfortunately when we do this, before long we realize that we have turned in the wrong way or to the wrong things, because wherever we turn, the unhappiness is there. It is then that we try to appear holy, spiritual, concerned, sincere, supportive, in love, loving, level-headed, visionary, disciplined, straight, gay, married and involved, single and available, mad or unhappy, or happy, nice, etc. However, at the end of our efforts we are still unhappy because we cannot outrun our hearts.

My heart ensures that my unhappiness and my condemnation is continual, and though I have looked for an anecdote to help me cope and have searched for a remedy of inner peace, I have found nothing except myself in this courtroom of life. I am on trial with my heart as the chief witness against me, using information against me; information that is unresolved and unshared.

As my heart begins to speak, I wish I were the person described by the unnamed ancient Jewish writer who said, "Happy is the man whose own soul does not condemn him." It is when I hear the testimony of my heart that I realize that in many ways my heart is right. I have been trying not to deal with the unresolved hurt by acting like it would just go away. I have not tried to address the real issue. Instead I have been trying to blame others and have even been trying to return hurt for hurt. In fact, if I am honest about it, that is why my relationship is so messed up right now. It's because I am trying to make someone hurt for my hurt. Even if it's a new relationship, my motto is: Though you didn't do it, somebody has to pay for it.

I have been trying to out-hurt my hurt. I mean, since they cheated on me, I will cheat on them more. I heard my name on the gossip line, so I will talk about more people. I rape because I was raped. My parents ignored me, so I will pay them back by not loving my kids. My daddy beat me, so I'm going to fix him—I'll beat my kids. She walked out on me and I didn't resolve it, but I will show the next girl. This is the testimony of the heart that is on the stand, and the truth of the matter is that it could be any of us in that courtroom.

But I have learned that you will never be able to out-negative the negative. You cannot out-hate hate. You cannot out-murder murder. How are you going to out-sex sex?

You will never feel better about him or her leaving you when you leave someone else, because once again you are alone. Breaking someone else's heart does not change the fact and hurt of your heart being broken. You cannot spend the hurt away.

This is a powerful truth, and the musings of this testifying heart resonate with the thinking and feelings of that vendetta type of resolution that screams, "Somebody has to pay, and it has to be somebody's fault." My heart is condemning me and the pain won't go away. Everywhere I go, it follows like a stalker. So in my heart

I try to out-condemn my condemner. This is where the needless break-ups and the "I'm not happy anymore" syndrome originate. The switching of relationships and people like underwear comes from this same place. This is where the verbal and physical abuse stems from. This is the area where Baby Mama Drama and Gold Digging come from, and the address where the *Desperate Housewives and the Men Who Make Them Desperate* live. It is at the intersection of Unresolved Hurt and Unshared Pain.

It is also at this intersection that the text shows up. It says that even when our hearts condemn us, God is greater than our hearts because he knows all. This beautiful text reveals the motive and the essence of the pressure and pain of self-condemnation. The pressure and the pain of self-condemnation is that fearful fact that we are the only one who knows what our heart knows and we must keep it a secret. The problem is that the people from whom we try to hide it have no power to rescue us from the pain and pressure of self-condemnation. In fact, the truth be told, they will add more weight to us.

But the shout is that there is someone else who knows everything that our heart knows: every sin, shortcoming, statement, thought, habit, desire, lust, lie, etc. But not only does He know what our heart knows and uses to condemn us, God is greater than our heart, and He alone can love the hurt away.

15

Courage Under Fire

When Jesus had finished saying these things, he left Galilee and went down to the region of Judea east of the Jordan River. Large crowds followed him there, and he healed their sick. Some Pharisees came and tried to trap him with this question: "Should a man be allowed to divorce his wife for just any reason?" "Haven't you read the Scriptures?" Jesus replied. "They record that from the beginning 'God made them male and female.' And he said, 'This explains why a man leaves his father and mother and is joined to his wife, and the two are united into one.' Since they are no longer two but one, let no one split apart what God has joined together" (Matthew 19:1-6, NLT).

It is a war of unprecedented proportions. A conflict, if you will, of the sorts that mankind was definitely not ready for. Though there was no formal Presidential request nor was there a formal Enactment and Declaration of War from Congress, this war continues as we stand, as we sit, and as we speak right now. Please know that this war is not one that started recently. No. In fact, in a real sense it pre-dates all of the atrocities of the wars we have seen. Yes, this war's origin stretches back before the illegal and unjust war in Iraq and Afghanistan. It started before the bloody ethnic cleansing that our United States government ignored in

Rwanda in 1994, where 1,000,000 Hutus and Tutsis were killed. It goes back before Vietnam and Korea and even before the Holocaust of Germany, which only pales in comparison to the Middle Passage of African slaves as the most heinous act against mankind. This is an age-old war of unprecedented proportions. A conflict, if you will, of the sorts that mankind was definitely not ready for, and a war it is.

War is defined as the reciprocated, armed conflict between two or more incongruous entities aimed at achieving a subjectively designed geo-political desired result. What is this original undeclared war, one that rages as we stand, as we sit, and as we speak? It is the war that started on that fateful evening near the beginning of time when God Himself passed out judgment on Man, Woman, and Serpent. And the enmity was made even greater between mankind and the tempter Satan and seemingly, in an undeclared fashion, war has waged between the enemies of God and those who keep the covenant of God.

We know this to be true, of course, in the tempting of the saints and those who endeavor to keep the covenant of salvation. It is a war that Satan strategically wages not only externally but also internally, which means that there is a war that wages between our spirit and flesh. Furthermore, this war is waging against the covenantal relationship of marriage. In fact, in a real sense the collateral damage of this war is at an all-time high. This can be seen in the staggering statistics that almost 60% of new marriages end in divorce. If that is not enough, there are some who suggest that, in the statistics concerning marriages among Christians, the percentage is even higher—near a staggering 70%!

Wow, can you believe it? An institution founded by God's people rooted in their interpretation of God's word is seemingly the underdog against the enemy, with the point spread not favoring the people of God. God's folk, who having the power to sing, shout, preach, speak in tongues, cast out demons in church and in public on Sunday, Tuesday, and Wednesday, don't have or don't exercise the power of patience enough in private and in the covenant that they are in with their spouse. As a result, the war indeed rages like an unchecked California brush fire whose constant fuel from the stream of the winds seems both unrelenting and unceasing.

Like any war, you expect there to be shots fired from both sides. Is not that what war is? The fact that you have a viable and most times visible enemy, one with whom you are knowingly at war and they who are knowingly at war with you; isn't that war? You know that they don't like you, and they know that you don't like them. That's war! When we are in war, you are shooting at me and I am shooting at you. I am trying to advance both my geographic position as well as my political and economic prowess. I am fighting for the control of your stuff and your power while maintaining a stronghold on my own. In war I am shooting at you, scheming against you to see how much I can advance my efforts and my agenda, and I expect you to shoot back.

Only in our crazy American psyche, so drunk and/or high off the Alizé of arrogance, while overdosing on the white lines of the flag do we expect to shoot at other peoples and countries around the world and for them to not shoot back. Think about it. We get offended that another country has the audacity to get upset and garner their military resources to fight back against the geo-political moves we have made on their soil to advance freedom and preserve liberty. We call our soldiers who do that patriots, but when they protect or avenge what's theirs we call many of them terrorists.

Outside of that American pipe dream, however, is the truth that when you are in war you expect people to fight back. In fact, you want them to fight back; after all it is war. They are on that side and you're on this side, competitors if you will. What you would never expect and never imagine in a million years is the fact that some of the onslaught of fire that you are taking is not coming from behind the enemy lines after all. The thing that knocks the wind out of you and is the most heartbreaking is that in this war in which you and your spouse are trying to defeat the enemy, the one who is trying to destroy your covenant, is that the fire is coming from your side. You are being bombarded by friendly fire; those who should be the main ones on your side—your parents, children, family, and friends—are shooting at your marriage.

When you are under this type of fire, will you have the where-withal to continue to fight for the interests you believed in when you made vows at the altar? Will you have the strength to stick to your original subscriptions that you went with into the war even when the war heats up? Will you still fight for what's right even when bullets are flying, bullets that feel so wrong because they are being shot from your side of the fight? Will you have courage under fire even when it's friendly fire that you're up against?

Jesus was on his way from Galilee and headed to Jerusalem for the last time. We know from the Gospels that he grew up in Nazareth, which was in the region of Galilee, and he had been to Jerusalem at least three prior times. This is seen as Luke the physician shares with us that when Jesus was 12 or 13 years old he travelled to Jerusalem and got lost, and after his parents searched for three days they found him in the church. John's penned testimony tells us that Jesus had been to Jerusalem at least two other times for the Feasts of the Passover and Unleavened bread. This time was different because this was the last time that he would travel there. Luke gives us a prophetic and theological hint when he proclaims that Jesus set his face steadfast toward Jerusalem. In essence, Luke says that Jesus set the whole of his presence, His face, on a crash course with his purpose being Calvary. It was on his way there that the Pharisees who are tempting him confront Him with the hot topic of that day, divorce.

You see, Herod Antipas, the King of the area, has stunned every-one by marrying his late brother's wife, with whom he'd had a long-term affair. The two leading schools led by Rabbi Shammai and Rabbi Hillel, in a political move, released two opposing views to the press. Shammai held to the traditional belief that adultery was the only reason for an acceptable divorce, while the school led by Rabbi Hillel believed in the liberal view that a man should be able to divorce his wife for any reason possible.

It was with this query that they cornered Jesus and asked him what his teaching on the subject was. Jesus said, "Haven't you read the Scriptures? They record that from the beginning 'God made them male and female.' And he said, 'This explains why a man leaves his father and mother and is joined to his wife, and the two are united into one. Since they are no longer two but one, let no one split apart what God has joined together.'"

As I have shared with you before, I like Jesus. They were there to confront and embarrass Jesus and He asked them, "Haven't you read the Scriptures?" The Pharisees were experts in the Scriptures, and with one question Jesus basically, as the young people would say, fronts them with their own material. He asks if they had read the Scriptures and begins to give them a Sunday school lesson. He does this by asking the following, "Wasn't it God in the beginning that made male and female? This explains why a man shall leave his mother and father and cleave to his wife, and the two have become one and no longer shall they be two. What God has joined together let no man put asunder or separate."

Even while these words of Christ ring and resonate at every wedding, the war between the enemies of God still rage against the keepers of the covenant of God, and if we are honest, we expect that fire. However, what catches us off guard and what is most heartbreaking, as stated, is that most of the fire we take does not hail from enemies, and if we peer closely at the words of our Christ we are able to see from whence the friendly fire comes.

You see, marriage is to be fellowship, intimacy, and communion. A set table, if you will, for those who are invited to be with one with another and even those they trust enough to share in their feast and life together, these being family and friends who will be able to share in affirmation and confirmation at this set table which represents fellowship between the two in covenant. The man and the woman are united in a feast for life, united as one. They are expecting an onslaught from the enemies of God, the kind of fire that comes from behind enemies' lines. But too often the fire comes from those whom they have invited to the table—mothers and fathers, children and other family members, as well as friends who have been invited to the table.

They have been invited as spectators and celebrators, not haters, to witness and walk with this union, but oftentimes these alliances with both husband and wife end up providing friendly fire that wages against the marriage. Furthermore, without proper boundaries those invited to the table can be detrimental to the success of the covenant relationship. Lest you misunderstand me let me clearly state that these people can and should be the healthy and needed community for a marriage to faithfully grow and mature. These trusted persons ought be invited to the table to share the successes and bright days like graduation, the announcement of pregnancy, the birth and blessing of a child, etc. They are also those who have helped and prayed during some of the tough times, like the death of a loved one, sickness, loss of a job, etc. In fact, in a real sense, it is these fellowships that sometimes are the only things that get you through.

But it is from their point of reference at the table that the friendly fire as an ever-present danger looms nigh. Because if you are not careful as they share with you and yours about yours or about theirs, without the proper perspective and boundaries, there can be transference of influence that can begin to outweigh, clutter, and subtract from the purity, the intimacy, and the communion of the marriage. This inclusion that can be either inspiration or infiltration is done primarily through the practice of "triangling."

Triangling is when the two people who are in covenant at the table invite the others at the table to serve a more intimate role at the table than the one in which they have covenant. This is done when they feel that they cannot or will not be heard by their spouse, and they seek validity to and affirmation of their thoughts, position, and/or agenda. This validity that they seek most times is the validity or attention that their spouse for whatever reason was not giving. As a result, they will invite someone else in, which is easier than doing covenant work. Instead of honoring the marriage covenant, others are given a larger and more active role.

This happens when the father and/or mother of the married couple have been invited to sit here at the table, and the parents begin to talk to their children more and more. The parents begin to talk to their daughter or their son more than the spouses themselves talk, and if there are no boundaries, the alliance between child and parents begins to overshoot the covenant with spouse.

"Haven't you read the Scriptures?" Jesus replied. "They record that from the beginning 'God made them male and female.' And he said, 'This explains why a man leaves his father and mother and is joined to his wife, and the two are united into one. Since they are no longer two but one, let no one split apart what God has joined together.'"

This revelation may be controversial in some circles, but the parent/child relationship is not seen in the eyes of God as covenant, spousal relationship is. However, oftentimes this is not understood even after marriage has begun.

A husband can't be a husband and a momma's boy at the same time. A wife can't be a wife and a daddy's girl at the same time. If an argument happens and the wife says I'm going home to my mother or my daddy always told me I could come home, in this instance, the wife is being a better daughter than a wife. This is when your marriage is under fire from those who were designed to help. It's called friendly fire, and when it hits there is a need for courage under fire.

Then you have the children. Children are huge targets for triangling. Of course, this is when the parents, who for some reason are not getting along with their spouse, invite the kids into subject matter that should be above their pay grade. This is seen the most in mixed families, a home that has stepparents and children. In times of pain the biological parent of the children will triangle off the children against the stepparent. Parents may turn to triangling to get an audience with the kids in order to somehow give validity to their position and/or agenda, which is super-unhealthy because it makes kids who most times are bound by emotions for both parents to have to spilt their loyalties and affections. Though most times this is not the desire of the parent, it causes pain. This is when there needs to be "courage under fire" enough to not to include the kids.

Finally, it is the friends. These are the non-family relationships that have most likely lasted a lot longer than the relationship between the hosts of the table. Since the husband and wife have not known each other as long as the friends, they believe that there is an unwritten code that the spousal relationship is a second-level operation to the friendship. The sharing of sensitive, intimate, and even sexual material that should not be shared, as well as if the friend outside the marriage is of the opposite gender, compounds this tension and war. The best way to remedy this problem, though it is painful, is to end all relationships that try to position themselves above the covenantal relationship of marriage. Friendships are not covenantal outside the marriage vows, and when they try to position themselves as such, they set themselves as the enemies of God.

The enemies of God will sometime wreak havoc on the covenantal marriages of the people of God. Furthermore, the proverbial table of fellowship that marriage represents can and sometimes will be left in disarray. The promise is that the covenant can be strained but it is never easily broken. That truth is in the declaration of Jesus Christ where he says, "What God has joined together let no man put asunder." Two things speak loudly from this particular text. The first is the fact that Jesus said "what" God put together and not "whom" God put together. The institution of marriage in the sight of God is more important than the personalities and feelings of the couple. The second thing is the fact that God is the One who should have put it together. This marriage is more than just a good idea; this is something that the Lord made. God has a vested interest in what God joins, and when God does so it cannot be easily torn asunder.

It is through God's love that even after parents, children, family, and friends have torn up your table of fellowship, intimacy, and communion—it is after you have wanted to quit but stayed in the covenantal faith—that God will invite you back to the table. This time, though, it will just be you, your spouse, and God. It is there that God will set the table and the table will only be Bread and Wine. And if you want, there between you two, God will defeat the enemy and restore covenant.